Disciples at the Crossroads

Disciples at the Crossroads

Perspectives on Worship and Church Leadership

John F. Baldovin, S.J.
Donald M. Clark
Peter E. Fink, S.J.
Kathleen Hughes, R.S.C.J.
Mary Ann Jordan
Richard P. McBrien
Gilbert Ostdiek, O.F.M.
John R. Page
Paul J. Philibert, O.P.
Elaine Ramshaw
Evelyn Eaton Whitehead
James D. Whitehead

Eleanor Bernstein, C.S.J., Editor

A Liturgical Press Book

The Liturgical Press
Collegeville, Minnesota

Cover: Design by Ann Blattner. *Illustration:* "Jesus at Emmaus" by Rembrandt.

1 2 3 4 5 6 7 8 9

Library of Congress Cataloging-in-Publication Data

Disciples at the crossroads : perspectives on worship and church leadership / Eleanor Bernstein, editor.
p. cm.
Includes bibliographical references.
ISBN 0-8146-2146-5
1. Catholic Church—Liturgy—Congresses. 2. Christian leadership--Catholic Church—Congresses. I. Bernstein, Eleanor.
BX1970.A1D57 1993
264'.02—dc20 93-591
CIP

For my parents, Philip and Theresa

Journeys now ended, theirs is the kingdom . . . .

Contents

Contributors

John F. Baldovin, S.J., is associate professor of historical and liturgical theology, Jesuit School of Theology and the Graduate Theological Union, Berkeley.

Donald M. Clark is pastor of St. Augustine and St. Monica parish in Detroit and past president of the National Black Clergy Caucus.

Peter E. Fink, S.J., is associate professor of sacramental/liturgical theology, Weston School of Theology, Cambridge.

Kathleen Hughes, R.S.C.J., is professor of liturgy at Catholic Theological Union, Chicago.

Mary Ann Jordan is a clinical psychologist in private practice in New York City and adjunct assistant professor in the Graduate School of Religion and Religious Education at Fordham University.

Richard P. McBrien is professor of theology at the University of Notre Dame and former chair of the department. He holds the Crowley-O'Brien-Walter Chair in theology.

Gilbert Ostdiek, O.F.M., is professor of liturgy at Catholic Theological Union in Chicago and member of the advisory committee of the International Commission on English in the Liturgy.

John R. Page is executive secretary of the International Commission on English in the Liturgy.

Paul J. Philibert, O.P., is prior provincial of the Southern Dominican Province and past president of the Dominican School of Theology, Berkeley.

Elaine Ramshaw is assistant professor of pastoral care and counseling, Methodist Theological School in Ohio, Delaware, Ohio.

Evelyn Eaton Whitehead is a developmental psychologist, lecturer, and author.

James D. Whitehead is a pastoral theologian, lecturer, and author.

Acknowledgments

Without the diverse gifts of many persons, books such as this one may never come to be. I gratefully acknowledge first the contributions of the twelve speakers whose papers are included in this volume. By their participation in the Notre Dame conferences and subsequent preparation of a written text, they support the much needed dialogue between theology and pastoral practice. May their numbers increase! Thanks also to Lorraine Strope for her dedicated secretarial assistance and to Johan van Parys, whose careful eye assured the accuracy of troublesome footnotes. But if there were no conference in the first place, surely there would be no papers to edit. To the staff of the Center for Pastoral Liturgy: John Brooks-Leonard, Nathan Mitchell, Barb Dudley, and Lorraine Strope, my deepest gratitude. Each year it is their hard work, generous commitment, and enthusiastic spirit that make the conference happen. For their dedication, may God be praised!

Introduction

The title of *Disciples at the Crossroads* evokes that memorable gospel passage of the two disciples who met a fellow traveler at the crossroads as they made their way to Emmaus, the traveler who managed in the course of an evening walk to capture their imaginations and take hold of their hearts. The subject of that engaging conversation, as you recall, was current events—"the things that have happened in Jerusalem in these days . . ."

In *these* days—and months and years—of pilgrimage following the Second Vatican Council, how many of us have longed for an experience like that of Cleopas and his companion, to walk along the road a piece with that engaging rabbi from Galilee, to hear him reflect on "the things that have happened in *these* days". No doubt, sincere disciples would speak their concerns for the life and growth of the Church, "and we had hoped that *this*" (i.e., the Second Vatican Council) would be what would redeem the church of Sacramento or St. Paul, of Honolulu or Halifax. The exchange might turn to issues of ministry, to the changing face of leadership, and perhaps even to Sunday celebrations in the absence of a priest.

There is, I submit, as much truth as poetry in that imaginative scenario. The image of Christ and the disciples on the road is an image of the Church at any time in its history, the Church that continually seeks to understand why Christ had to suffer these things, the Church that in dialogue with that rabbi must grapple with questions of leadership and ministry and Sunday celebrations, with present demands and future challenges.

The twelve essays that follow originated as presentations at two liturgical conferences sponsored by the Notre Dame Center for Pastoral Liturgy, *Ritual and Pastoral Care* and *Disciples at the Crossroads*. The papers explore the "eternal" questions that affect the growth and development of the Church in any age: leadership, sacramental celebration, ritual authenticity, and religious meaning in what is often perceived as an alien culture.

In making this material available to a broader audience, it is our hope that the fruitful exchange begun at those gatherings on the campus of the University of Notre Dame may continue, in parishes and schools, in colleges and seminary classrooms, wherever and however the gospel ministry brings disciples together.

Eleanor Bernstein, CSJ

Richard P. McBrien

The Church at the Crossroads

It is both an honor and a privilege for me to address this opening session of the Nineteenth Annual Conference sponsored by the Notre Dame Center for Pastoral Liturgy. The theme of this year's conference is "Liturgical Leadership in the Church of the 1990s." As the conference organizers so aptly remind us, we are "disciples at the crossroads"—followers of Jesus Christ in search now of new leadership for a new decade and, sooner than we may realize, for a new century and a new millennium.

We live in a time that sociologist Alvin Toffler referred to twenty years ago as one of "future shock." Jules Verne's late nineteenth-century science fiction fantasies are today's technological realities, and the developmental process continues to accelerate.

Toffler observed that if the last 50,000 years of human existence were divided into lifetimes of approximately 62 years each, there have been about 800 lifetimes. Of these 800, 640 were spent in caves.

Only during the last 70 lifetimes has it been possible to communicate through the written word, and only during the last 6 has humanity had access to the printed word. Further, Toffler was writing before the computer revolution of the 1980s, with its high-speed laser printers and desk-top publishing programs.

Only during the last 4 lifetimes have we been able to measure time precisely, and only in the last 2 have we had the use of an electric motor.

Even within our own lifetime we have seen the world pass from agriculture as the primary form of human labor to the so-called white-collar labor of salespersons, administrators, educators, communicators, etc. Indeed, the term "knowledge industry" would have made no sense at all to our grandparents and even to most of our parents.

Advances in transportation show the same kind of delayed—and then highly accelerated—change. In the year 6000 B.C. the camel caravan, at eight miles per hour, provided the fastest means of travel over long distances.

Not until about 1600 B.C. did the invention of the chariot increase our capacity to 20 MPH, and that mark wasn't surpassed for several thousand years.

Not until the nineteenth century, with improvements in the steam engine, did we reach speeds of 100 MPH; it had taken the human race thousands upon thousands, even millions, of years to do it.

Only fifty-eight years later, however, planes were breaking the 400 MPH figure, and in another twenty-five years even that seemed modest, as the new jets doubled the record.

By the 1960's rockets were approaching speeds of 4,000 MPH, and astronauts were circling the earth at 18,000 MPH. In the same decade we reached the moon and soon thereafter sent pilot-less probes to the outer planets. Indeed, in the summer of 1989, Voyager II streaked past the planet Neptune and one of Neptune's moons, Triton (three billion miles from the earth) sending back computer-enhanced photographs of stunning clarity. Launched more than twelve years ago and moving at some 38,000 MPH, Voyager II was only four and a half minutes off schedule as it passed over the second farthest planet from the sun!

Yesterday's impossible dreams in the field of politics and human freedom are also becoming the unbelievable realities of our modern world. Who would have guessed, just six or seven years ago when the Solidarity movement was outlawed and many of its leaders in prison, that today a leading Solidarity intellectual would be serving as Prime Minister of the Polish government—and with no Soviet tanks in sight? Indeed, who could have imagined, back in the days when President Reagan referred to the Soviet Union as "the evil empire," that the Soviet Union itself would have a leader being compared with the late Pope John XXIII or that he would have generated across the face of Europe and more recently here in the United States a new form of political enthusiasm known as "Gorby fever"? For John XXIII it was *aggiornamento*, updating, for the Catholic Church. For Gorbachev, it is *glasnost* and *perestroika*, openness and restructuring, for the Soviet Union. Can any of us say that she or he expected the kind of open upheaval we observe today in the Baltic states of Estonia, Latvia, and Lithuania, or in Moldavia, or in Azerbaijan, or in Armenia, or in the Ukraine, with its restive population of some fifty million? And what of the dramatic events throughout the rest of Eastern Europe? In East Germany, with the opening of the Berlin Wall and the move toward unification with West Germany, in Czechoslovakia, Hungary, Bulgaria, and even Romania? 1989 may be remembered as the most momentous year in the entire twentieth century. But then, again, who knows what the century's last decade holds for us?

We have experienced profound change and have come to expect even greater changes in technology and politics as we stand on the threshold of a new decade, a new century, and a new millennium. But we know, also from our experience, that religion has not been exempt from the phenomenon of "future shock."

"These new conditions have their impact in religion," the Second Vatican Council declared some twenty-five years ago in its Pastoral Constitution on the Church in the Modern World, *Gaudium et spes.*

"On the one hand, a more critical ability to distinguish religion from a magical view of the world and from the superstitions which still continue to circulate purifies religion and exacts day by day a more personal and explicit adherence to faith. As a result," the council observed, "many persons are achieving a more vivid sense of God."

"On the other hand, growing numbers of people are abandoning religion in practice. . . . As a consequence, many people are shaken" (GS 7).

We live in a time, therefore, of crisis, a time, literally, of coming constantly upon new crossroads and of being compelled to make difficult choices. Which way to turn? Which road to follow? We are truly now, perhaps more than ever before in the history of the Church, "disciples at the crossroads."

We fumble with our maps. We squint into the sun at the unfamiliar road signs. We look desperately around for a reliable source of directions. We check the gas gauge. We glance at our watches. Who shall lead us, indeed?

A time of crisis is, literally, a time of decision. That is the root meaning of the Greek word for crisis. The experience of crisis is the experience of uncertain travelers at a crossroad. No one is more welcome at moments like these than people who are informed and knowledgeable, people who exude a sense of purpose and who inspire confidence, people with a sense of direction and the capacity to guide us "in right paths," as the psalmist put it. We look, in other words, for evidence of authority—authority not as domination, however, but as true leadership.

But because any authority involves power, we cannot afford to be naive about it. Power is the capacity, for good or for ill, to influence, shape, and at times *control* our thinking and our behavior.

Karl Rahner once defined power as "a certain self-assertion and resistance proper to a given being and hence as its innate possibility of acting spontaneously, without the previous consent of another, to interfere with and change the actual constitution of that other" ("The Theology of Power," *Theological Investigations,* 4:391). Rahner states what is self-evident: that each of us, simply because we exist, has power in a certain sense and to a certain degree. Each of us has the capacity to do or to say something that affects another or not to do so.

Rollo May offers a straightforward definition in his book *Power and Innocence.* For May, power is simply the ability to cause or prevent change. He notes five kinds of power:

1. *exploitative* power, the most destructive because it presupposes violence or the threat of violence and leaves no choice at all for the victim;
2. *manipulative* power, exercised over another in subtle and often unconscious ways and, thus, without the explicit consent of the other and often against the other's best interests;
3. *competitive* power, employed against another, although not necessarily against the other's best interests;
4. *nutrient* power, exercised for another, as by a parent or some magnanimous public official;
5. *integrative* power, exercised with and for the other, in complete harmony with the other's interests and desires. The greater the love and the greater the commitment to justice, the closer one approaches integrative power.

Power, therefore, may be good, bad, or indifferent, depending on the way it is used. Applied for the benefit of others and ultimately for the sake of the reign of God, as in the case of integrative power, it is a force for good. Applied against the interests of others and ultimately against the reign of God, as in the case of exploitative power, it is a force for evil.

The same is true of power in the Church. There is nothing wrong with power in itself; what is at issue is the *use* of power. Even if there were something inherently wrong with power, we would have to live with it anyway since, as Rahner reminds us, we cannot avoid it as individuals, nor can we avoid it as a community. By its very nature, the life of a community requires some interaction of wills in pursuit of some common goal or purpose. Even when those wills are in harmony, power has to be exercised in one way or another. When they are not in harmony, power conflicts result.

Rollo May's typology is readily applicable to the Church. *Integrative* power, i.e., power exercised out of love and a sense of justice on behalf of others and in the interests of others, makes collegiality work and is the reality which makes Christian community possible. Indeed, we speak of the "power" of the Holy Spirit, who is the ultimate principle of *koinonia*, or community. *Nutrient* power is exercised by Christian parents, to be sure, but also by many who fulfill some pastoral ministry in the Church. It is not as ideal for the Church as is *integrative* power because it implies an inferior-superior relationship, as in the case of a bishop who presumes to act as "father" to his priests, some of whom may be his own age or older. Where *nutrient* power is exercised when *integrative* power is called for, *nutrient* power is a negative, not a positive, force for the Church.

Competitive power, i.e., a power used against another to advance one's own interests, likewise can be either good or bad. It is good when it promotes the success of the best qualified minister or the best conceived pastoral project. It is bad if it is used unfairly, even in the achievement of a good end, if it is used only for the attainment of more power for its own sake, or if it is used to advance unsuitable people or programs.

Manipulative power, i.e., the subtle exercise of power over others without their consent, is almost always bad, especially when exercised in the Church. Manipulative power can be justified only in relation to subjects who cannot make sound judgments and decisions for themselves. By definition, these are children or seriously immature adults—neither of whom are supposed to be models for understanding the composition and responsibilities of the people of God. Unfortunately, some Church officials place all the laity in the category of children or seriously immature adults and label them "the simple faithful."

Exploitative power, which uses force or the threat of force against others, is never justified within the Church, which is not to say that it does not exist in the Church. It exists, for example, where workers in Catholic institutions are denied their natural right to organize or are paid below-standard wages and fringe benefits. Exploitative power exists where individuals are compelled to remain in certain ministerial roles under the threat of serious damage to their reputation, peace of mind, or their capacity to earn a living. Exploitative power exists where individuals are denied their full rights—personal, social, economic—because of their sex or their race. Force and violence come in many forms, other than physical.

POWER AND AUTHORITY

Thus far, we have considered the various forms of power. Power is what makes authority work, and this, too, for good or for ill. What does authority mean? Is it *juridical authority,* i.e., the legal power to enforce changes of behavior in others, or the power to judge what is true and what is erroneous, what is right and what is wrong? What of *de facto* authority, sometimes called "moral" authority? Is *de iure* authority necessarily of a higher order than *de facto* authority? Who has exercised more "authority" in the Catholic Church these past few decades: Mother Teresa or her archbishop in Calcutta? Dorothy Day or Cardinal Spellman? And who was shown to have had more real authority in the early 1960s, following the heated debates over religious liberty: the once-silenced Fr. John Courtney Murray, or his principal adversary, Cardinal Alfredo Ottaviani, prefect of the Holy Office and a predecessor of Cardinal Ratzinger? Obviously, *de facto,* or moral, authority is more significant than *de iure,* or official, authority. When the two are combined, however, the result is an even more compelling example of authority, as in the case of Pope John XXIII.

And what of the manner in which authority is exercised? The model for Christian authority is Jesus himself. The Gospels record that he spoke and acted as one having authority; indeed, "all authority, in heaven and on earth" was given to him (Matt 28:18), and all creation is subject to him (Phil 2:10). And yet Jesus exercised his authority in the manner of a servant (Mark 10:45; Luke 22:27). It is precisely because he did not cling to his divinity that he became Lord of all (Phil 2:5-11). Thus he charged his disciples, then and now, to follow his example: "Earthly kings lord it over their people. . . . Yet it cannot be that way with you. Let the greater among you be as the junior, the leader as the servant [*diakonos*]" (Luke 22:25-26; John 13:14-15). His disciples, he insisted, were not to be engaged in any struggles for power or preferment among themselves (Matt 20:20-28; Mark 10:35-45).

And what of the range and limits of that authority? The absolute power Jesus claims in Matthew 28:18 is not transferred to his disciples. Not even Peter receives it. In Acts 1–12, where Peter's leadership is most clearly portrayed, decisions are made by "the Twelve," or "the apostles," or "the Church," and not by Peter alone. His action in Acts 10 is reviewed by "the party of the circumcision," the counterpart of our own Catholic traditionalists. James, not Peter, presides over the Council of Jerusalem. Peter's devious behavior at Antioch elicits an open rebuke from Paul (Gal 2:11-14).

Nor are the apostles (and their "successors") the sole participants in Jesus' authority. There are also prophets, teachers, wonder-workers, evangelists, presbyters, and others (1 Cor 12:28; Eph 4:11). When Paul was criticized, he never appealed to his ecclesiastical status as a basis for immunity from criticism. Indeed, he recognized that the Spirit is given to the whole Church, and not just to its leaders (1 Cor 12:1-28; Rom 12:3-8). There is a diversity of gifts and charisms, and all must work together as one for the good of the whole.

A NEW KIND OF AUTHORITY

Because true Christian authority is rooted in the Holy Spirit, and not in ecclesiastical office, it is of a unique kind, not precisely definable by sociology, canon law, or even ecclesiology. Christ has given his Church a new kind of authority.

In the Catholic tradition, so deeply sacramental at its core, the Church, at whatever level and through whatever ministers, exercises authority most effectively only when it actually practices what it preaches, or more precisely, when it practices what Jesus preaches. This is a matter of fundamental principle. The First Vatican Council declared that the primary sign of credibility is the holiness of the Church itself. We teach, first and foremost, by example.

Christian authority, therefore, must always be *de facto*, or moral, authority. It can never rely solely or even principally on the exercise of force or official power. When the Christian authority-figure has to resort to threats and censures and penalties, he or she has already lost authority.

Furthermore, because the Church is the whole people of God, authority and power reside in the community as a whole, although exercised in various ways, by various persons, for the good of the whole. Authority and power are always and everywhere to be exercised in the manner of Jesus, who was among us as one who serves (Mark 10:45). Authority and power which are detached from holiness, i.e., from Christian wholeness or integrity, are not *Christian* authority and *Christian* power. Authority and power which seek to coerce place themselves above the grace of the Holy Spirit, and so are not authentically Christian.

The Church, the people of God, comes into being through conversion, the free response of individuals to the call of God in Jesus Christ by the grace of the Holy Spirit. The Church, therefore, is a community of disciples. Authority and power in such a community can be exercised only in ways which respect the freedom of the act of faith and the voluntary character of discipleship.

Finally, the Church is essentially a missionary community, committed as Jesus was to the coming of the reign of God, a reign of justice and peace as well as of holiness and grace. Authority and power, therefore, are always eschatological in nature: they exist always in the service of the coming reign of God and never as ends in themselves. The Church's work for the sake of God's reign involves proclamation, worship, witnessing, and service. Authority and power exist in the Church to promote and to facilitate those missionary responsibilities, and to hasten the coming of God's reign.

WHO SHALL LEAD?

We are "disciples at the crossroads," asking the question, "Who shall lead us?" Ultimately, of course, it is the Holy Spirit who will lead us. More immediately, however, it will be those members of the Church who manifest the necessary gifts, or charisms, of the Holy Spirit for the task of leadership. Who discerns the presence of those gifts? Each individual Christian community does, for each community is the Church in a given place; and the Church, at both universal and local levels, is the whole people of God, not the hierarchy alone.

Richard P. McBrien

What kind of leaders are we to look for in the 1990s and beyond? The Business section of the Sunday *New York Times* (June 3, 1990) recently carried a pertinent article on the subject, entitled "A New Understated Kind of Power." The author, Robert Dilenschneider, noted that business leaders in the 1980s loved to flaunt power. In his estimation, that day is now past. (One thinks not only of junk bond entrepreneurs like Ivan Boesky and Michael Milken, but also of Donald Trump.) Nineties power, Dilenschneider writes, will be very different. Business people will still exert power and influence, but they will do so in a very different way. Business is under greater scrutiny now, from federal, state, and local governments at home and abroad, as well as from the financial community at large and from their own employees.

The effective use of power for the 1990s, according to the *Times* article, is becoming a new management science, with its own axioms and rules. Dilenschneider offers five axioms by way of example. They can be applied to power and management within the Church as well; I will offer some brief applications.

1. *Make change an ally.* Change is as inevitable as it is threatening ("future shock" again). Good leaders must communicate its promise and its positive aspects, and help interpret it for their people.

Likewise, the Church does not need leaders who oppose change, or who dwell on its dangerous and risky aspects. The Church needs leaders who can read the signs of the times and who exude a sense of confidence in the Spirit's action in history.

2. *Gather intelligence relentlessly.* Power and influence depend on information. Effective leaders must do their homework. They cannot afford to be misled by specially commissioned studies, but must constantly scan other, independent sources of information in the public realm.

Likewise, the Church doesn't need leaders who supinely defer to the Vatican or to "higher authority" even on matters in which they and their fellow Catholics enjoy special competence.

3. *Use your symbolic role.* Dilenschneider notes that when the Monsanto Company evolved from a standard-issue chemical company into a business reliant on advanced technologies, its chief executive officer spent time in the laboratory learning the new nature of work in the organization.

Likewise, Church leaders cannot remain above and beyond the field of pastoral activity. The Church's "business" is pastoring. The

Church's leaders must be, first and foremost, pastors, with pastoral, not organizational, hearts. In the Church, one cannot lead people on the basis of a rule book or of hard-line directives from on high. The Church ministers to human beings, and human beings are too rich and too complex to be programmed by rule books or controlled by administrative decree.

4. *Create an agenda.* Have a short list of four or five major issues and focus your energies on them. Many effective leaders spread themselves too thinly and try to do everything. The result is that their messages lack priorities and their words fade into the vast sea of information.

The Church, too, needs leaders with a sense of vision and a sense of priorities. First things first; last things last. With the many problems we face as a Church and as a nation, problems associated with housing, poverty, education, health care, aging, drug addiction, violence in the home and on the streets, hopelessness, alienation, and loneliness in the world, the Church does not need to spend time, energy, and resources on a new Universal Catechism. Nor does it need to seek out new, and equally ineffective, ways to harass Catholic politicians over the issue of abortion.

5. *Take the high road.* The Ivan Boesky, Michael Milken, and Donald Trump days are over. American competitiveness demands strong values at the workplace. Power, Dilenschneider concludes, no longer means privilege.

Likewise, the Church needs leaders for the 1990s who, like Jesus, are service-oriented, not office-oriented or status-oriented or privilege-oriented. The Church's leaders exist to serve, and not to be served. Like Jesus.

Such leaders already exist in the Church. In some few cases, they occupy or have occupied important ecclesiastical positions and their names are well-known: Archbishop Rembert Weakland in Milwaukee, the late Cardinal John Dearden in Detroit, Pope John XXIII. But in most cases such leaders hold no major ecclesiastical office; they wear no special vestments; they carry no croziers; and their names and good works are known only to their own people in their own local parishes and dioceses. They are directors of religious education, directors of youth ministry, directors of worship, parish council presidents, pastors, social action ministers, writers, teachers, counsellors. And they are as likely—indeed more likely—to be female as they are to be male.

Richard P. McBrien

Who shall lead us? The Spirit. And where is the Spirit? In the Church, among other places. And who is the Church? *You* are the Church. *We* are the Church.

We are faithful disciples of Jesus Christ at the crossroads, looking for leaders. And they are us!

James D. Whitehead

Worlds of Scarcity: Promise of Abundance

In these post-Vatican II decades which have witnessed dramatic changes in so many areas of Church life, Catholics have found themselves adjusting (with greater or lesser ease) to a reforming and renewing Church. The ecclesial life we have lived in the 1970s and 1980s is unarguably different from the experiences of our parents. The Second Vatican Council was a watershed in Church history; how easily we apply the designations pre-Vatican II and post-Vatican II. As we stand at the threshold of this last decade of the millennium, we face what may be the greatest challenge yet of this post-Vatican II era. Some call the challenge a crisis—a crisis of scarcity.

Parishes are consolidated for lack of priests. Catholic hospitals and schools shut their doors, victims of escalating operating costs. Diocesan budgets shrink. These diminishments on the outside cause shudders on the inside. As their numbers dwindle, many priests question the meaning of their vocation. Those who work for the Church confront their own inadequacies: lack of stamina and resilience; rising doubts. Throughout the Church a mood of loss and diminishment grows.

As a gospel people we are marked by paradox: we follow Jesus who found life in death and success in the midst of defeat. It should not be surprising, then, that in this season of loss and purification, a time of "shortages" can be a time of abundance.

We look at the frightening lack of priests in local parishes and see that because of their absence hundreds of able and generous persons come forward ready to serve the Church. Until now the priests' strong presence had hidden these surprising resources. Although fewer and fewer Catholics "go to confession," reconciliation *is* happening in our communities. In recovery programs, Marriage Encounter, and faith sharing groups, Christians struggle to heal deep and lingering wounds. The thirty-five-year-old man who no longer goes to regular confession instead struggles to heal the anger that has separated him for decades from his father. The forty-four-year-old woman, instead of her weekly visit to the confessional, strives with a counselor to heal the shame that lingers from sexual abuse in her childhood. The sacrament of reconciliation epitomizes the paradox of our life of faith: we live simultaneously in scarcity and abundance.

THE INVENTION OF SCARCITY

To understand better this mystery of absence and plenty, we look more closely at our wants and needs. Scarcity is often genuine: poverty, illness, homelessness are real deprivations. Yet while scarcity is a painful fact, it may be more apparent than real, more illusion than reality. A neighboring town lacks food, but our granaries are full. Do we live in scarcity or abundance? A Rolex watch and BMW car are valuable because they are scarce. To ensure their value, we must take care that they remain in short supply. Scarcity is, at times, a human invention! In the peculiar economy of the human spirit, we assign scarcity a special value. Consumerism is the societal addiction that trains us in this illusion of scarcity and need.

If this "invention" of scarcity occurs in cultural life, we may also expect to discover it in religious life. Christians invent scarcity when they seek to control and manage God's grace, when they curtail the profligate outpouring of the Spirit. When leaders decide that lay persons should not preach, they make the good news scarce. When the Church limits ordained leadership to unmarried men, it guarantees that the sacraments will be in short supply. When a parish agrees that the priest should bear all the responsibility, it creates an artificial scarcity.

The temptation to make God's grace scarce is best represented by the theological judgment, now happily abandoned, that "there is no salvation outside the Church." (Imagine God's surprise upon hearing this!) With this inventive statement, Catholics sought to reduce God's extravagant grace to official channels. They intended to make grace scarce, captive to institutional guidelines.

THE POWER OF LEADERSHIP: SCARCE OR ABUNDANT?

In a season of scarcity we reexamine our life of faith in search of abundance. How have we invented our own scarcity? How do our visions of community and leadership sap our faith and diminish God's grace?

Christian leaders in the twelfth century defined priesthood as the power to perform the sacraments. For the first time in the

Christian tradition, the Church began to picture ordained leaders as having a power that was lacking in the community. The priest, it was imagined, possessed the power to *do* the sacraments, with or without a community. His special power of leadership was disengaged from the community.

This vision of leadership made power scarce. Henceforth the priest and bishop were solely responsible for the sacraments. Communities of faith became deeply passive, convinced of their scarcity of power.

In this present climate of diminishment, is the scarcity real or have we invented it?

In the Gospels the common word for power is *dynamis*: a dynamic of energy that moves through a group to heal or injure it. This dynamic may be the power of hope that guides a group through a crisis; it may be the shared rage that binds a community in its hatred of its enemy. Power is not a "thing" that strong individuals possess, but a social dynamic that energizes a community. In the New Testament this *dynamis* is what goes on among those gathered in Jesus' name. It is another name for the healing power of the Spirit.

In chapter eight of his Gospel, Luke relates the story of Jesus and his friends moving through a crowded street. A woman who has been ill for some time tries to get close to Jesus. Unable to get his attention, she is just able to touch his clothes as he passes. Jesus stops and asks: "Who touched me?" His friends remind him that many people have bumped against him as they edge their way through the crowd. But Jesus adds, "I felt power flowing out of me." The woman's touch has released the power of God in him and it flows through him to heal her illness. Jesus does not decide to dispense some power that is his personal possession. The woman's touch taps the *dynamis* that is the Spirit in Jesus and it moves through him to heal. This power becomes scarce only when we are out of touch with Jesus; in contact with him, we find it in abundance.

The account of Pentecost is the central story of God's *dynamis* surging through a group of believers. The passage begins as a story of scarcity: Jesus' death has left his friends feeling impotent and defeated. Gathering in an upper room, the disciples are overcome with grief. Suddenly, some unexplainable energy, the power of the Spirit, stirs among them. A new mood of hope and confidence energizes the group. This unexpected and abundant power unites and galvanizes them in a new and lasting way.

There are no individual heroes at Pentecost; this is not a celebration of the apostles or other leaders. In this feast we recall the power of God enlivening a whole community. A scarcity of hope among the disciples is transformed into an abundance of faith.

Each of us has experienced this. For example, a small group of Christians gathers to pray. Sometimes, in the midst of their sharing, they are moved to a new level of forgiveness and faith. Breaking bread, they are nourished in surprising ways. The leader did not cause this; he or she arranged the meeting, hoped for something special, but is still amazed when the power of God stirs through these folk in such a healing way.

Such experiences reveal the gospel vision of power and leadership. Leaders, both ordained and non-ordained, are called to orchestrate this abundant power of God. Leaders manage, critique, encourage, and arouse a group's energy. They do not *provide* God's power to a group, as if they uniquely possessed this grace or delivered it. This saving *dynamis* was present in the community long before the leader arrived and will be there after the leader is gone. For a short time, a leader orchestrates, like a guest conductor, this surprising and abundant power of God's grace.

CONFLICTING VISIONS OF LEADERSHIP

Our worlds of scarcity and the gospel promise of abundance come into conflict in our visions of Christian leadership. In one traditional vision, we see the ordained leader acting in ways that we cannot. The priest makes Christ present in the Eucharist, forgives sins in confession, heals the sick in the sacrament of anointing. We see the ordained leader as having a special power that we lack. In this vision of leadership we create scarcity in two ways. (1) Because the leader has absorbed all priesthood, we never talk of a "priestly community." We forget the New Testament conviction that we are a priestly people. Priestliness, restricted to ordained leaders, becomes scarce. (2) We picture God's grace as in short supply. The ecclesiastical leader alone has access to this scarce power. If the lay person gains power (to preach, to teach catechism, to make financial decisions on the parish council), this comes at the expense of the ordained leader. One Christian's gain in power is another's loss; turf becomes very important and we protect our little area of power and influence, instead of sharing it. We create, in the midst of abundant grace, domains of scarcity.

In another vision of leadership, we see the leader doing things to remind us that we do them too. The leader's presiding at the Eucharist reminds us that we make Christ present in our homes and offices. The sacrament of reconciliation reminds us that we are to be forgiving in our daily life. The sacramental oil of anointing reminds us of our healing touches with sick children, dispirited friends, aging parents. If we perform none of these holy and powerful actions, we should not expect the sacraments magically to transform our worlds of scarce grace.

Leaders, ordained or not, invoke God's saving power to remind us to do likewise. When they act this way instead of clutching the sacraments as their private domain they help make power abundant. Reminding us of our vocation, they multiply power. The word goes out: power is not in short supply; there is enough to go around. And we begin to speak again of a priestly community.

These two visions of power—as scarce or as abundant—are enacted in a single hospital. On the seventh floor, a person lies dying, surrounded by many family members. The chaplain arrives and spends some time listening to the family's grief. Then the chaplain announces, "If you will all step back, I will now anoint Helen." The anointing and invoking of God's grace on the person is the work of the chaplain.

On the third floor of this same hospital, another Christian approaches death, again with his family members surrounding him. The chaplain comes into the room and spends some moments speaking with the family members. Then the chaplain announces, "If you will all step forward, we will anoint William." The sacramental anointing and calling of God's grace upon this person is the vocation of all of us. We perform this powerful action together. The official leader still leads: this person has brought the oils, initiates and guides the ritual, and is recognized as representing the Church. The leader's action reminds the group of its abundant power to touch and invoke God's blessings on the one who is sick.

PRIESTLINESS: SCARCITY AND ABUNDANCE

The most painful diminishment in our Church today is in the priesthood. The decreasing number of vocations and the malaise among priests themselves suggest that perhaps God is transforming this venerable gift to Christian life. God is transforming the priesthood by breaking it. In order to purify and recast this role of leadership, God breaks it open. The fruit of this painful change is that we glimpse the core of priesthood: our common priestliness.

In the First Letter of Peter (2:9) we read that we are a priestly people. "But you are a chosen race, a royal priesthood, a holy nation, God's own people, that you may declare the wonderful deeds of him who called you out of darkness into his marvelous light." Priestliness pertains first to a community of Christians. What does it mean for a group to be priestly?

Priestly actions announce abundance. Communities and individuals act in a priestly fashion when they announce the abundance of forgiveness and nourishment. A group acts in a priestly fashion when it witnesses, by its life, that forgiveness is possible. In a world long on grievances and short on reconciliation, Christian communities remind us that forgiveness is still available, in abundance. A community of Christians, by the way it lives, announces nourishment. However alone or starved or addicted or malnourished we may be, this group holds out a promise of nourishment. Ordained leaders serve and guide groups that perform these priestly functions. We call these leaders priests because they minister to a priestly people. Ordained leaders are to remind us of our priestliness, instead of relieving us of this responsibility.

Priestliness announces abundance; clericalism witnesses to scarcity. Clericalism and priesthood are not at all the same thing. As a recent study published in *Religious Life at the Crossroads* says, clericalism "is neither identical with nor a necessary consequence of priesthood, but a diminishment and distortion of it."

A religious leader, ordained or not, who has succumbed to clericalism makes power scarce. Such a leader guards a personal privilege and turf. Structures shaped by clericalism restrict the access to ministry; they exclude others from service. Clericalism seeks to absorb all the priestliness in the community, leaving others passive. Leaders shaped by clericalism insist "this is *my* parish!" Service becomes status, ministry becomes privilege; and grace is made scarce.

Each of us knows priests who act in a very priestly way. The way they preside at the Eucharist encourages our participation; their leadership in the parish evokes our responsibility. Power is increased and made abundant. Each of us also knows ordained and unordained leaders who cling to their authority. Unable to share power, they make it scarce.

In this season of scarcity, we recognize clericalism as an ornate cloak that has been wrapped around priesthood. For centuries this garment seemed to protect the priesthood and give it a certain status. These days we are engaged in a most delicate operation: unwrapping this protective cloak from the Christian priesthood. As we do so, we catch glimpses of priestliness, the vocation of every Christian to witness to abundance.

ABUNDANCE IN JESUS CHRIST

In this current crisis of scarcity and abundance we turn again to the gospel and the witness of Jesus. "I have come so that they may have life and have it abundantly" (John 10:10). One day Jesus had been speaking to a very large crowd. The hour grew late and Jesus became aware that they must be very hungry. But his disciples remind him of the logistical problems: "Where could anyone get bread to feed these people in a deserted place like this?" In this land of scarcity, Jesus asks his friends to search the crowd for whatever resources are available. When these are blessed and shared, there is enough to feed everyone. "They ate as much as they wanted, and they collected seven baskets of the scraps left over" (Mark 8:8). Fragmented resources, held in private, are turned into bountiful nourishment.

In Jesus Christ, God has given us great abundance. Can it be that we, the Church, have invented scarcity? If that is so, then the recovery of God's abundance must begin with us, called to be a priestly people. It is precisely as a priestly people that we must reimagine power and leadership. In that process, we will re-claim our vocation to be a chosen race, a royal priesthood, declaring the wonderful deeds of the One who called us out of darkness into marvelous light.

NOTE

Whitehead Associates, 1990. A further discussion of this paradox in Christian life can be found in *The Promise of Partnership: Leadership and Ministry in an Adult Church* (San Francisco: Harper Collins, 1991).

James D. Whitehead

Evelyn Eaton Whitehead

Exploring the Leader's Task

Most traditional cultures give leaders an elevated status: mounting the regal throne or ascending the high altar, the leader stands above the people, superior to others in the community. Jesus, however, urged his disciples to resist this interpretation of leadership and, in his own life, modeled an alternative: "The greatest among you must be your servant. Those who exalt themselves will be humbled, and those who humble themselves will be exalted" (Matt 23:11-12). His leadership reached its height in his paradoxical elevation on the cross.

From the outset, the Christian community has stumbled in its efforts to live up to this extraordinary ideal of leadership, often succumbing to cultural pressures to interpret leadership in the community of faith in terms of privilege and status. Only recently, for example, have we moved beyond the titles "Your Eminence" and "Prince of the Church." Throughout the Middle Ages popes invoked the title "servant of the servants of God" even as the papal office became increasingly monarchical and authoritarian. Today, as the Christian body moves toward greater partnership in faith, our formal leaders come down from their pedestals. Nevertheless, the ministry of leadership continues to be one of special responsibility. How then should one describe the particular authority of our servant leaders within the Church?

It is helpful to admit at the outset that most Catholics today find the image of servant anachronistic. In the contemporary cultural imagination, "servant" too easily translates into servitude, even slavery. The service of leadership that Jesus demands, however, arises not in a master/slave economy but within a community of disciples. Although the concept of servant can suggest powerlessness, leaders must be powerful, strong enough to initiate action, to confront obstacles, to speak the truth, and to console those in pain. How can this image of servant be reconciled with the demands of the leadership role? Another gospel image—stewardship—points the way.

In the New Testament a steward is an authoritative servant. In the gospel and elsewhere, stewardship is a leadership position reserved for experienced, capable persons. The steward oversees the domestic order, the rhythms, rules, and agreements by which a household or community thrives. Stewards exercise considerable authority, but not in their own name. Stewardship links power with service (of the community) and authority with dependency (on the Lord). These dynamics describe the exercise of leadership in the contemporary community of faith.

STEWARDS OF THE GROUP'S SPIRIT-POWER

Christian leaders are stewards of God's power as it stirs in a community of believers. Leaders are not to *do* the group's work nor single-handedly to *supply* the group's vision. They do not impart a grace and power that is otherwise lacking. Their role is to *support* the group's life in the Spirit. Their task is to foster the network of effective relationships through which members care for one another and pursue shared goals. When they do this, leaders foster the flow of God's power within the community.

The truth borne by the gospel images (as well as the insights of sociology) points to the core of leadership: bringing the group to life and coordinating its power. Leadership—or better, leading—happens in the give-and-take of the whole group. Such interplay envisions leadership as a group process more than as an individual possession, a process that encompasses all those activities that make a group effective. In this model, the formal leader is part of a larger process. Far from doing away with the need for designated leaders, this wider view serves to clarify the task of the person in charge.

Theologian Annie Jaubert reminds us that in the earliest Christian communities leadership was seen as "the responsibility of all and the charge of some." What, then, is the charge of the formal leader? How does the person "in charge" serve the broader leadership process? While a leader's job description will differ from group to group, common expectations emerge. Effective leaders act (1) to nurture commitment, (2) to enhance the group's power, and (3) to turn the group toward its future.

LEADERS NURTURE COMMITMENT

Nurturing commitment means strengthening the emotional and intellectual bonds that hold a group together. A good leader does this by keeping the reality of interdependence before the group. Effective leaders reinforce the conviction that members need one another. By celebrating the successes and by recalling the dangers still to be faced, leaders remind the group, "we are in this together."

Commitment makes groups come alive, as people invest their talent and their needs. The group draws from the talents of its members the skills and experience that make it effective. But from members' needs, the group draws an even more important resource: commitment to common action.

Effective leaders help the group to recognize the truth that needs link us to other people. Other people share the same concerns. We soon realize that by joining together, *all* may achieve what *each* wants. Private interests are not set aside; they become part of shared hopes, and shared hopes stimulate shared goals.

Effective leaders thus draw people's needs into this common focus, and then tap this energy for action. By shaping separate interests into shared goals, leaders craft the common good. Personal goals and group goals overlap. People begin to interpret their own interests in new ways, seeing other folks not as competitors but as valued partners in a joint enterprise.

In order to help groups translate their shared hopes into practical goals, however, leaders must be at ease with conflict. The goals of a group do not pre-exist, fully formed but hidden, like buried treasure waiting to be discovered. Theologian Bernard Loomer reminds us that the common good is an emergent good. Antagonism among members, disagreement over the right course of action, resistance to change, competing demands on the group's limited resources—these are the ferment from which common goals emerge. Leaders who are afraid of conflict try to avoid the messy compromises that diversity demands. In doing so, they cut the group off from the emotional roots that generate commitment.

LEADERS RELEASE AND ENHANCE THE GROUP'S POWER

Good leaders release the power in others. They invite people to recognize their own gifts and offer these to the common task. For example, the parish RCIA director recruits members of the adult community to exercise this significant ecclesial ministry; the school principal initiates a faculty development program and encourages teachers to participate; the parish council devises practical ways for other parishioners to take on greater responsibility: these are leadership activities.

Leaders enhance the group's power by nurturing competence and exercising control. In most organizations, formal leaders carry management responsibilities, which involve overseeing other people in their performance of tasks. As manager, the leader supervises the group's resources—time and talent, machines and money, property and personnel. Effective leaders, however, do not only regulate resources; they make more of the group's resources by making it easier for other people to do well: By staffing—getting the right person in the proper job. By recruiting—enlisting new members to share the group's tasks. By training—expanding people's skills so that they can do a better job. By evaluating—providing constructive feedback to help people improve their work.

Effective leaders help groups devise workable strategies for making decisions, setting goals, dealing with conflict, and keeping each other informed. When the work is well organized, members know how their different responsibilities support the common effort. These practical procedures build the group's power, focusing its energy on shared tasks and common goals.

Leaders also carry responsibility for control—monitoring performance to keep it up to par, evaluating progress to insure that goals are met. Admittedly control has a bad reputation among us. Many have seen that administrative control too easily masks manipulation, especially in an organizational setting that lacks the safeguards of due process and mutual accountability. Checking the dictionary, however, we find that the definitions of control include "bringing together a number of resources," "keeping a complicated effort on track," "giving a sense of direction to a larger effort"—all tasks essential to effective collaboration. Without this kind of control, group effort easily dissipates. Energy evaporates as decisions are delayed and resources wasted.

The exercise of control does not have to be manipulative: recall the power of the conductor in an orchestra or the director in a play. Each role requires control, the ability to focus a group's energies, to channel diverse resources into an organic whole. For the group to be effective, the leader, too, must exercise control, but the leader's control exists in context. The goal of the joint effort—a successful performance—lies beyond the leader's singular ability and provides the criterion by which his or her action can be judged. Both the group and the leader are accountable to something beyond themselves: the script they all follow. Both the conductor and the musicians know the score. This metaphor illumines the context of control in religious leadership. In the Church today more and more of the members have access to the script—scripture, tradition, history, theology—and more and more know the score—the political implications of ecclesial life. This makes leaders accountable to the community psychologically even when they are not yet accountable to the community in the structures of organizational life.

When organizational control is exercised in pursuit of a common goal and in the context of mutual accountability, the temptation toward manipulation can be resisted. Then it is safe to welcome the control function back into corporate life—safe for both formal leaders and the community.

LEADERS TURN THE GROUP TOWARD ITS FUTURE

While most organizational leaders have management responsibilities, managing and leading are not the same. Management activities focus primarily on implementation: supervising people in the accomplishment of designated tasks; coordinating resources for the achievement of existing goals. Few organizations function well without this concentration on the task at hand, but management activities can have other effects as well.

In some groups, the implicit goal of management becomes stability: maintaining the current patterns of organizational life. In pursuit of efficiency, the manager prizes good order and internal harmony. The manager's job is to follow a plan already in place, not to encourage innovation. In such a setting, management and leadership are at odds.

Although both managing and leading involve influencing people in the pursuit of common goals, there are important differences. Leaders do more than supervise subordinates; they recruit people to construct the future together. Vital organizations acknowledge that the people in charge have the dual responsibility of administration and transformation. Administration supports organizational stability; transformation helps the group confront the demands of change. Some organizations, unfortunately, downplay the leader's responsibility for change, defining the person in charge as essentially a guardian of the status quo. Limiting the leadership role in this way undermines the leader's legitimacy and erodes the whole group's effectiveness.

Leadership moves beyond coordinating plans already in place to activating a vision adequate for the future. Transformation is essential to the leader's job. Effective leaders engage the group not just in accomplishing tasks but in formulating a shared vision. Formulating vision is a complex and volatile undertaking. Previous convictions come under review. Questions of the group's meaning and purpose arise. Resources of imagination and hope, until now bruised or buried, come to life. Once begun, the visioning process can seldom be held within the boundaries of "the way things are."

Effective leaders, aware that current arrangements may not be adequate to the future, encourage openness to change. Sometimes the change takes the shape of reform. The leader calls the group together to evaluate procedures and policies already in effect. The intent is not to overturn the current vision, but to find better ways to accomplish it. Sometimes the group's active participation in visioning has a more radical effect. As the group dialogues about values and needs, a new vision emerges, one that questions the adequacy not only of current procedures but of current goals as well.

Leaders empower groups for transformation. Transformation puts higher priority on growth than on organizational maintenance. Transformation does not repudiate the past simply because it is past, but always questions the present, exposing the gap between "what is" and "what could be." Walter Bruggemann, in his evocative book *The Prophetic Imagination*, explores the connection between conflict and transformation.

Prophetic leaders, Bruggemann states, help us "see through the present." For most, the present is a vision filled with daily activities and responsibilities, duties and distractions. When the present, with all its pressing needs and engaging delights, absorbs our attention, we easily miss the hints of God's future already active here and now. Prophets challenge the status quo, the way things are. For religious folk, it takes about twenty years for the way things are to become the way things have always been, and another hundred years for the status quo to become God's immutable design from all eternity.

Prophetic leaders invite us to reexamine the assumption that God favors the status quo. Bruggemann uses a wonderfully sinister term to describe the status quo; he calls it "the royal consciousness." The prophets of the Hebrew Scriptures, Bruggemann observes, questioned the royal consciousness, challenging the royal arrangement. The royal arrangement today proposes a universal catechism to contain the living faith of a multicultural world-wide Church. It excludes from full sacramental leadership women and those who are married to women. It calls an international synod on the laity and neglects to include the laity as full participants.

Organizational renewal and institutional transformation challenge the royal arrangement. They provoke controversy as they clash with parts of our past. Effective leaders learn to accept conflict as a necessary, even valued companion of transformation. In the pursuit of growth, conflict is a surprising ally.

Conflict comes, however, with a bad reputation; our religious heritage has often connected controversy with sin, conflict with disobedience, dissent with disloyalty. Some of us carry wounds from dysfunctional families, where we learned to link conflict with blame and shame. Common sense, then, often concludes that conflict feels bad and has negative results. Yet, even as we nod in assent, most of us recognize that this negative judgment does not tell the whole truth.

We look back on personal experiences where struggle strengthened us. We recall friendships in which a conflict faced deepened the relationship, while a dispute covered over had disastrous results. In his now-classic book *Leadership*, James McGregor Burns, the eminent historian of the American presidency, reminds us that "leaders, whatever their profession of harmony, do not shun conflict; they confront it, exploit it, ultimately they embody it." Whatever their personal hesitancies, effective leaders learn to welcome conflict's energy, to harness its power, to focus its purpose, and to discern its contribution to the future we share.

We stand at a time in our history as a Church when the careful re-examination of the tasks of leadership can have enormous consequences for the future. The challenge is to seize the moment, aware that leaders are stewards of the group's Spirit-power with a responsibility to nurture commitment, to release and enhance power, and to turn the group toward its future.

NOTE

Whitehead Associates, 1990. For an extended treatment of the understanding of leadership offered in this chapter, see James D. Whitehead and Evelyn Eaton Whitehead, *The Promise of Partnership: Leadership and Ministry in an Adult Church* (San Francisco: Harper Collins, 1991).

John F. Baldovin, S.J.

Liturgical Presidency: The Sacramental Question

In his 1971 novel *Love in the Ruins*, subtitled *The Adventures of a Bad Catholic at a Time Near the End of the World*, the late Southern Catholic novelist Walker Percy painted a grim but comic picture of the Church of the future. Near the beginning of the novel, the hero, Dr. Tom More, says:

> Our Catholic Church here split into three pieces: (1) the American Catholic Church whose new Rome is Cicero, Illinois; (2) the Dutch schismatics who believe in relevance but not God; (3) the Roman Catholic remnant, a tiny scattered flock with no place to go. The American Catholic Church, which emphasizes propertyrights and the integrity of neighborhoods, retained the Latin Mass and plays the *Star-Spangled Banner* at the elevation.
>
> The Dutch schismatics in this area comprise several priests and nuns who left Rome to get married. They threw in with the Dutch schismatic Catholics. Now several divorced priests and nuns are importuning the Dutch cardinal to allow them to remarry.
>
> The Roman Catholics hereabouts are scattered and demoralized. The one priest, an obscure curate, who remained faithful to Rome, could not support himself and had to hire out as a fire-watcher.[1]

I begin with Percy's vision not because it is now the reality, but because, as only a creative artist can do, he imagined even twenty years ago the possibilities and the perils of a Church experiencing a new and dizzying sense of freedom. While Percy's vision may not be true today, it is naive to imagine that the forces he describes are not at work in the Church. I set my remarks within this somewhat apocalyptic context in order to highlight the seriousness of the question before us. If the Church is not to split asunder, then sane, balanced, and rigorous thinking must be applied to the issue of liturgical leadership. We must consider: (1) what is the nature of liturgical leadership in the context of the Church's ministry? (2) who may exercise this leadership? and (3) what happens in a eucharistic assembly when ordained leadership is not present? (This includes the problem of communities that disregard the traditional notion of ordination.)

It is necessary to situate these questions within a contemporary understanding of Church since liturgical leadership is essentially related to ecclesiology. Therefore, before confronting the question of the relation between ordination and liturgical presidency, we need to consider first, the purpose of the Church and second, the nature of sacramental activity, in particular the Eucharist.

MINISTRY AND THE CHURCH

One of the primary reasons that liturgical presidency has become a pressing issue for us today is the radical shift in ecclesiology articulated at the Second Vatican Council and confirmed in the experience of the grassroots Church in subsequent years. We have experienced a major transformation from the image or model of the Church as a perfectly ordered hierarchical society, in which grace and divine power flow from the top down as in a pyramid, to one in which the assembly of baptized believers as the people of God stands at the center. Although a number of models of the Church are held in tension in Vatican II's Dogmatic Constitution on the Church, the more communitarian notion of the people of God, buttressed significantly by an insistence on conscious and active liturgical participation, especially as this has been expressed in the Rite of Christian Initiation of Adults, has inspired a radical shift in perception of what it means to be a Catholic Christian.[2]

We have recovered a vital sense of "baptismal dignity," the respect and honor due to each and every member of the Church. And although there is room—even necessity—for differentiated roles in the Church (with the inevitable differentiation of power), there is no basis for differentiating according to status in the Christian community. That is to say, all ministries exist for service, not as mere human honors.

Throughout its history the Church has struggled (often unsuccessfully) with the temptation to accommodate itself to purely secular notions of leadership and power, despite the rather clear evangelical injunction of Mark 10:43-44, "Whoever would be great among you must be your servant and whoever would be first among you must be slave of all,"[3] and the Pauline principle of baptismal equality in Galatians 3:28 where there is no room for distinctions based on ethnicity, social status, or gender. To put the matter plainly: one can no longer argue that God's Spirit is communicated to all the members of the Church solely through the channels of an official or hierarchical ministry, or rather, one can no longer mount such an argument without entering into considerable theological debate. The post-Vatican II revolution in ecclesiology centers on the insight that the Spirit works through the entire Church.

Without this move to a more biblical and communally based ecclesiology, contemporary trends in Catholic thought (such as the various political and liberation theologies, as well as theologies of inculturation and the feminist critiques of the Church) would have no starting point. It is impossible to over-emphasize the importance of the liturgical renewal in this process, which is what makes the liturgy such a point of contention. As the most clearly expressed symbol of the Church's experience and belief, the liturgy serves as the focus of every significant element in Christian faith, from the very idea of God to ethical behavior. When one connects the idea of active liturgical participation with the concept of the Church itself as a sacrament, i.e., a vehicle for proclaiming God's activity in Christ rather than the "ark" of the saved,[4] one has a radically different approach both to Church membership and to liturgical experience.

This notion of the sacramentality of the Church relativizes any claim the Church may have to being the sole realization of the reign of God. It therefore shows that the Church is to serve as a symbol of the unity of the human race as well as of unity with God.[5] Little wonder, then, that unity has been a prime concern for Christians from the very beginning. One of the functions of the ordained ministry has been to symbolize that unity both through leadership of local communities and communication between communities, as the Faith and Order Commission of the World Council of Churches has pointed out in its landmark convergence document, *Baptism, Eucharist and Ministry*.[6] A major element in symbolizing the Church's unity has been the continuity of ordained ministry with the apostolic witness, what has been traditionally referred to as apostolic succession. On the other hand, Edward Schillebeeckx has pointed out[7] that in the past too much emphasis has been placed on a mechanical notion of continuity through the laying-on-of-hands to the neglect of the preservation of the faith of the whole community witnessed by its ordained ministers. Moreover there has been a tendency in Catholic theology to identify the handing on of apostolic succession through the imposition of hands with an objectified definition of power, and thus to see a direct transmission of power from Jesus to the apostles to their successors. The roots of such a concept can be traced as early as the second century in the attempt of Irenaeus of Lyons to safeguard orthodoxy, the unity and authenticity of the Church's faith, by listing the succession of bishops in important Churches. Within recent history the critical study of the New Testament and of primitive Christianity has questioned the presumption that Jesus intended to found a Church in all of its organizational details. Scholars have shown that up until the late second century the threefold ordering of the ordained ministry into bishop-presbyter-deacon was far from universal.[8] In fact, even the Church of Rome seems to have known a more collegial governance by a council of presbyters (i.e., without a single bishop at its head) until the middle of the second century.

Thus we can conclude that there are two basic ways to understand the development of the forms of ordained ministry: first, as the gradual unfolding of the divine will, such that "by divine institution" the threefold ministry of bishop-presbyter-deacon was always what Christ intended; or second, that although the Church has always been served by office bearers, the shape that ministry takes has conformed to the needs of the Church at any given time and in any given culture. Because of the shifting interpretations given even to the three forms of ordained ministry the latter understanding seems the more probable.

Thus we can draw some conclusions with regard to the nature of the Church: (1) The ordained ministry is one of the basic ways in which the Church's unity is expressed; (2) The forms that such ministry takes should be related to the culture and historical situation in which the Church finds itself; (3) The role of ordained ministry must be related to the role of the Church as a sacrament or symbol of the salvation of the entire human race, with the Church itself understood as the Spirit-filled people of God. Part 3 will develop the implications of these conclusions.

MINISTRY AND SACRAMENT

Before exploring further the relationship between ordained ministry and liturgical leadership, some presuppositions about the nature of sacramental activity itself, in particular the Eucharist, must be clarified. How one understands sacramental activity fundamentally affects this relationship. There are two basic approaches. In one, sacraments are channels of grace from God to a fundamentally ungraced world; they are the vehicles of God's condescending mercy by which the faith of the Church and of individuals within it is strengthened. In another view, however, sacramental activity arises out of a world that has already received God's self-communication or grace. Therefore, sacraments act not, as it were, from above but from within the world and the Church is the sacrament of the world's salvation. This is Karl Rahner's lasting contribution to the contemporary theology of the liturgy.[9]

These approaches represent the chasm which exists in Catholic theology today, a chasm which runs from the doctrine of God to the theology of the Church and sacraments and extends to moral theology as well. Bernard Lonergan has named this the difference between the classical and modern worldviews.[10] I maintain that the first (or classical) approach is not tenable in a world which we experience as filled with divine activity both within and beyond the Church. In the latter (or modern) approach, then, sacramental activity serves as a focus of God's activity in everyday life. This approach by no means minimizes the importance and even necessity of liturgy but rather situates it within the wider compass of divine activity. In fact, far from denigrating the importance of liturgy, a focus on sacramental activity highlights the role of liturgy as the clearest communal expression of Christian faith and the existential response of faith in ritual activity. In other words, liturgy, or sacramental activity, "works" not so much by transferring grace to those who do not have it as by enlivening, or "fermenting," the grace-filled faith that already exists in the baptized. One's attitude toward the nature and function of ministry, both the ministry of the ordained and all other forms of Christian ministry, is profoundly affected by how one conceives God operating in the world. If one sees the divine activity as an intrusion from outside the world, then ministry will inevitably be the communication of grace to the great mass of the "unwashed" (with the pun on baptism intended). If, on the other hand, God is already at work in people's lives in the "profane" world, then ministry will serve to encourage and enable the gifts of the Spirit that are already present. Unfortunately, much of pastoral ministry is still predicated on the classic assumption that ministers are giving the rest of the community something they do not already have or telling them something they do not already know.

When one understands sacramentality as arising out of the lived faith experience of Christian people, the Eucharist is no longer a sacred rite performed by some (the ordained) on behalf of others who are powerless. Rather it is the self-expression of the body of Christ, head and members, made visible in a ritual manner. With this understanding, we can see that Catholic theology took a disastrous turn in the medieval period by separating the theology of the sacraments from commentary on the liturgy, as though the liturgical "envelope" were unimportant relative to the "essential elements" of the sacraments. Any contemporary theology of the sacraments, therefore, must take into account the way that the ritual activity symbolizes the presence and activity of God in the faith of the Church. The Rite of Christian Initiation of Adults reflects most clearly the understanding that sacramental activity is a process rather than the communication of some "quantity" of grace.

With regard to the Eucharist, the consistent and traditional Catholic insight has been that the community gathers on the Lord's Day to celebrate the Lord's Supper because in the Eucharist the community experiences itself in the most heightened ritual fashion as the body of Christ. This is by no means a purely external or arbitrary obligation but rather flows from the nature of the Church itself, ritually and symbolically expressing its union in faith by the sacred sacrificial meal which it understands to be the Lord's most precious heritage. The climax of this sacramental realization of being the body of Christ is the act of communion. Today we risk divorcing that communion from the enactment of the body of Christ in Eucharist. This is an understandable development, given the concentration of our piety and theology on the sacred elements of transformed bread and wine. In the process of defining and adoring the real presence of Christ in the sacred elements, however, we have (at least in the past) lost the intimate connection between the elements and the Church that consumes them. We have forgotten that body of Christ is as accurate a designation of the Church as it is of the transformed elements.[11]

Recall that we speak of a *transformation* of the Eucharistic elements primarily because the Eucharist is concerned with our ongoing transformation as the body of Christ. Furthermore, overemphasis on the act of communion represents an imbalance with regard to four other important aspects or meanings of the Eucharist so well treated in *Baptism, Eucharist, and Ministry*: namely, thanksgiving to the Father, memorial of the Son, invocation of the Spirit, and meal of the kingdom.[12]

The reason for this potential divorce today stems not only from an overemphasis on communion (which is after all related to a happy recovery since the time of Pius X) but also from the situation of churches which lack an ordained presbyter at the Sunday celebration, the question of so-called "priestless Masses." Our acquiescence to the theology and practice of Sunday communion services in the absence of a priest has nothing less than potentially disastrous consequences. As others have well pointed out,[13] divorcing the Sunday service from Eucharistic celebration is markedly untraditional and breaks the inherent connection between Sunday, assembly, and Eucharist. William Marravee puts the matter very well: "What in fact appears to be most characteristic of the present situation is that less importance is being ascribed to the integrity of the eucharist and to the eucharistic dimension of the local community than to the maintaining of a male celibate ordained ministry."[14]

Marravee's point is no exaggeration. He is referring to the same priority of Eucharist over ordained ministry that Edward Schillebeeckx has insisted upon when he writes that the community has more of a right to the Eucharist than the Church has a right to impose male celibacy as a condition for ordination to the presbyterate.[15] It is this insistence on limiting presbyteral ordination to male celibates that has created the anomalous situation of Christian communities without ordained ministers to preside at the Eucharist. Sunday communion services, then, in the absence of a presbyter are not making the best of a bad situation. On the contrary, they capitalize on a communion-centered piety and weaken the relation between Eucharist and assembly. They considerably weaken the body of Christ. What, then, is the relation between ordination and liturgical presidency?

ORDINATION AND LITURGICAL PRESIDENCY

On this topic, I begin by stating how important it is to be self-critical. Contemporary liberation and feminist theologies have pointed out that systems of thought can tend to be self-serving. Theologians like me (not to mention those who exercise official teaching authority in the Church) who are male, celibate, and ordained, must be wary of arguing in such a way that their conclusions serve some explicit or implicit interest in the status quo. Thus I will try to point out where I think this "status quo thinking" exists in current theological reflection upon ordained ministry. It may, of course, unconsciously be operative in my own treatment of the question. It is my hope, nonetheless, that an honest reading of tradition (in which I include the Scriptures as foundational) can liberate even male, celibate, ordained theologians from their most cherished ideological presuppositions.

First, ordained ministry and liturgical presidency must be situated within the context of the theology of the presbyterate; then the theological problems must be addressed; and finally the practical or pastoral problems in our liturgical experience vis-à-vis presidency must be named.

Throughout this essay I have deliberately refrained from using the term "priesthood" for the ordained presbyterate, on the basis of the complete absence of sacerdotal or priestly vocabulary in the New Testament itself, at least as far as Christian ministry is concerned. In the New Testament only Christ is priest of the new covenant; and the body of Christ, the Christians, is a priestly people.[16] Moreover, nowhere does the New Testament link presidency over the Eucharist to any specific minister, with the exception of Acts 13:1f. (where prophets and teachers preside) and Acts 20:7ff. (where Paul presides over the breaking of bread).[17] In fact it seems that employing the term *priesthood* for ordained presbyters clouds the issue, as Joyce Zimmermann has recently argued.[18] At least as far as the New Testament is concerned the entirety of the Christian people exercises a sacerdotal or priestly role in light of its unity in Christ. There can be no question of certain Christians bestowing blessings upon others simply in virtue of their office.

On the other hand, it is misleading to think of the earliest Christian communities as pure democracies of the Spirit or, as is often argued in some feminist theologies today, as a discipleship of equals.[19] Certainly the primitive Christians were equals when it came to being members of the body of Christ, but at least in Pauline thought they were differentiated with regard to charisms or gifts of the Spirit, as in I Corinthians 12. In other words, it is highly unlikely that leadership in worship devolved upon just anyone at all. Rather, it seems that the most fundamental meaning of ordination points to the community's designation of leaders who were found to be possessed of the Spirit of leadership. Such leadership was not primarily cultic or liturgical but rather communal.

Seeing the origins of Christian ministry in this way has two results: (1) it places liturgical leadership within the context of communal or ecclesial leadership; (2) at the same time it considerably relativizes notions of purely cultic ordination, as in the mistaken notion that Jesus ordained his apostles at the Last Supper, which is based on what Kenan Osborne has called a (faulty) ecclesiological presupposition.[20] Osborne distinguishes between two ecclesiological presuppositions: (1) the direct foundation and organization of the Church by Jesus himself; (2) the birth of the Church in the Easter experience of the disciples, who are filled with the Spirit. These presuppositions are similar to the classic and modern approaches to God's activity in the world outlined above. The first model (direct foundation by Christ) has been labeled Christomonistic in contemporary theological vocabulary, while the second has been called pneumatological.[21] It is the pneumatological model that understands the ongoing role of the Spirit in the organization of the Church and its ministry.

To sum up, then, the Churches represented by the New Testament documents knew a number of forms of leadership and charism but they do not witness to a cultic priesthood. In fact, strictly cultic (i.e., liturgical) forms seem to be radically questioned by the true form of worship which Paul sees as sacrifice of self in Romans 12:1, or which Jesus, in John's Gospel, claims will take place "in Spirit and truth" (John 4:23).

It did not take long, however, for roles within the leadership of worship to be stabilized. By the end of the first century the Didache shows glimmers of a transition from the itinerant ministry of prophets and teachers to that of overseers (or bishops) and presbyters in the presidency of the Eucharist. At the outset such leadership of the community at worship was conceived of collegially, as Paul Bradshaw points out. If a bishop presided, he did so as a member of a kind of governing board of the community.[22] This move toward stable structures did not seem to be problematic in and of itself. It is natural for a community of any longevity to establish structures and rules, in our case what is called "ecclesiastical office." But even as late as the early third century the first Latin theologian, Tertullian, was able to argue that the non-ordained could preside at the Eucharist in virtue of their baptism.[23] What does become problematic is the radical distinction drawn between clergy and laity that we observe in the fourth and fifth centuries.[24] Of particular importance in this development is the gradual adoption or re-adoption of ideas of purity with regard to the worship, ideas developed on the basis of typology from the religious faith of Israel. In other words, the Christian "priesthood" is likened to that of Israel, a radical departure from the New Testament notion of the priestly body of Christ.

The beginnings of clerical celibacy were certainly influenced by these Jewish ideas of purity as related to worship. While married men could become presbyters, they could no longer engage in sexual relations with their wives before they celebrated the Eucharist.[25] Doubtless this regulation mirrored the increasing Christian concern with sex and sexual abstinence that has been so well described by Peter Brown in his recent work, *Body and Society*.[26] Eventually celibacy became mandatory for the ordained in the Western Church with the Second Lateran Council of 1139. When this attitude toward purity is combined with the shift away from a symbolic to more objectively realist concept of worship in the early Middle Ages (i.e., concept in which the symbol and reality could mean the same thing), we arrive at what has essentially become the classic Roman Catholic approach to priesthood: the office is "ordered" primarily to the celebration of the Eucharist rather than to communal or pastoral leadership.[27] It is in part this sacralization of Christian life to which the Reformers of the sixteenth century objected.

Today the Catholic approach to theology of the presbyterate has shifted considerably. While at the same time affirming an essential difference between the priesthood of the faithful and the ministerial priesthood,[28] the Vatican II documents placed ordained ministry within the context of the threefold office of Christ as prophet, priest, and king. In doing so, the council stressed the preaching and leadership roles of the presbyter in addition to the cultic role, even though the priesthood is ordered to the Eucharist as its culmination. Ministerial leadership, then, is exercised in the Church not only through the expression of a kind of cultic power, but primarily through the preaching of the Word.[29] This model for ordained ministry places the liturgical role of the presbyter within the wider context of wholehearted service of the faith and of the faithful.

No doubt a tension will continue to be felt between what I have called the baptismal dignity of the people of God and the need for special roles of leadership in service of the community. What is most important, it seems, is that ordained ministry be conceived as the Church's recognition of the charism of leadership (for the Christian always expressed as service) and consequently the community's empowerment of leaders through ordination. As with any charism such empowerment is to be recognized as God's gift, not the creation of the community or of the individual who is called. At the same time this empowerment takes place on the basis of the perceived talent (charism) and preparation of the candidate for ministry. Always we want to avoid the granting of some kind of metaphysical power to the ordinand through the rite of ordination, loosed as it were from its moorings in the faith life of the community and the individual who arises from within the community as a leader.

A practical example serves to clarify this point. It is commonplace to "import" presbyters into parishes or other assemblies to which they do not really belong in order to preside at liturgical celebrations. Or, from time to time a presbyter visits a parish to which he does not belong and insists on his right to concelebrate in virtue of his status as someone who is ordained. In terms of the models I described above, these are aberrations. While it would be foolish not to allow of exceptions, e.g., a presbyter invited to preside or to preach in another community for some good reason, this should not be considered as normal practice.[30]

I have argued on the basis of consistent Christian tradition (1) that the Church needs ministers who are designated for service; (2) that this office can and has taken different forms throughout Church history; (3) that distinguishing too sharply between the status of the ordained and that of the baptised has been an unhelpful direction in Catholic theology and needs to be corrected. On the other hand, today we risk blurring the distinction of roles within the community and therefore within the liturgy. Two issues must be confronted: (1) who can be ordained? (2) what is the appropriate model for exercising leadership, particularly in liturgy?

First, who should be candidates for ordination to the presbyterate? The position that only male celibates are apt candidates for ordination in the Latin Church today is indefensible. There are absolutely no theological grounds for denying ordination to married men. Certainly the experience of the primitive Church (not to mention our sisters and brothers in the Protestant and Eastern Christian Churches) attests to this. The prohibition on married clergy can be argued only if sexual activity is perceived as somehow marring one's ability to pray. This has been the pious and theological attitude of Catholics since at least the fourth century and will not easily be transformed into a positive and healthy valuing of sexual activity without a great deal of effort. On the other hand, relaxation of the rule of clerical celibacy is essential if we are ever to communicate in any persuasive way the true baptismal dignity of all Christ's people. Moreover, as Schillebeeckx has argued,[31] the useful and valuable charism of celibacy will fail to be truly credible until it is made optional.

What then of the other side of this question about candidates—the admission of women to the presbyterate? Here we cannot argue so clearly from tradition, but we can see that the present position of the magisterium is based on certain ideological (or self-serving) presuppositions. I quote a paper circulated at the last synod of bishops by Joseph Fessio as a fair representation of the approach being taken by the magisterium:

> In the sacrament of holy orders God, through the instrumentality of those whom he has authorized to speak in the name of Christ, confers upon the sacred ministers the power to act in the name of Christ and in certain sacramental acts to act in fact as extensions of the one mediator, Christ. While the entire church is feminine and maternal, the clerical ministry within the church is by nature masculine and paternal. Because the bishop, the priest (and by participation, the deacon) not only represent Christ, but act as Christ in the eucharistic sacrifice of sacrament and word, only the masculine sex can represent sacramentally in an adequate way the male Christ who himself as male represents God facing creation and the bridegroom facing his bride the church. The church only becomes the body of Christ in the mystery of the two in one flesh by which, initially bride, by being joined to her groom, she becomes one body with the head. The eucharist, the center and summit of the sacraments, involves a sacred place, a sacred time and a sacred person both symbolically setting apart the orders of grace and redemption from the order of creation and sacrament. For this reason, many theologians (e.g. DeLubac, von Balthasar, Bouyer) hold in keeping

with a long and unbroken ecclesiastical tradition, that there is an absolute prohibition of women as recipients of the sacrament of holy orders.[32]

Here one finds essentially the same argument as in the "Declaration on the Admission of Women to the Ministerial Priesthood" from the Congregation for the Doctrine of the Faith.[33] There are several obvious flaws in Fessio's argument. First, he relies on an understanding of Christianity which I have called "classical": the sacred confronts the profane and transforms it; grace is not to be found in the act of creation itself. Second, and this seems always to follow from the first, he upholds the "ecclesiological presupposition" that Christ founded the Church and its organization in an explicit and conscious manner. Today, this is seen as an extremely doubtful position. Third, he raises the Pauline metaphor of the relation of Christ to the Church (bride and bridegroom) to the status of a doctrinal position. And fourth, on the basis of this abuse of metaphorical language, he argues that women are incapable of representing Christ. The language of representing Christ (or *in persona Christi*) has become commonplace in recent documents of the magisterium. I contend, first, that the fundamental ability to represent Christ is given in baptism to all Christians and not limited by gender; and second, that the very idea of such representation must always be contextualized within the Church (*in persona Christi*) which acts as one with its head as one Spirit-filled body.[34] On the basis of talent in leadership and ability to preach and to pray publicly, there is no tenable reason to refuse women as candidates for the presbyterate. I assume that on a profound level what is at stake here is both a deep and abiding fear of the feminine, especially in relation to the sacred, and an effort to maintain control over the sacramental system, a system that would inevitably change if women were ordained because the imaging of human beings in relation to the sacred would be completely transformed.[35] Perhaps our current "shortage" is not so much a lack of ordained ministers as a lack of courage to allow the Spirit to guide us into a truly contemporary form of Christian life and worship.

What then of the appropriate model for liturgical leadership in the contemporary Church? It would be not only untraditional but also naive to suppose that the Christian community could do without structure and leadership. Demythologizing or desacralizing this leadership and placing it within the context of the baptismal priesthood is not the same as doing away with it altogether. The real question becomes: how can liturgical presidency be "strong, loving, and wise" and at the same time more representative of the Church in contemporary culture? What is being called "co-presidency" or "shared presidency" may well be a solution to the problem of a perceived (even if unintended) domination over the liturgy by the presider. Such sharing of presidency is by no means untraditional. It occurred when bishops in the early Church ceded the Eucharistic prayer as a sign of hospitality to visiting bishops;[36] it occurs within the framework of the Roman Rite today when a bishop presides at the Liturgy of the Word, while a presbyter is designated to preside at the Liturgy of the Eucharist proper. It occurs as a matter of course when one presbyter presides in the Eucharistic or other liturgical celebration and another presbyter or deacon preaches. Perhaps shared leadership today can effectively symbolize the conviction that liturgical presidency does not mean domination but rather service.

There follow several practical or pastoral corollaries. The first relates to the current construction of the Eucharist in the Roman Rite. As Ralph Keifer pointed out insightfully some time ago a major weakness of the current Roman Rite Eucharist is that it is priest-centered rather than prayer or ritual-centered.[37] This is an unfortunate by-product of the change to the vernacular, the stance of the presider facing the people, and the liberties for more personalized expression at different points in the rite itself. The difficulty arises when presiders personalize the rite to the extent that they make it their own show. Even if their words are inclusive and progressive, the very activity succeeds only in drawing attention to themselves and away from the communal activity of prayer. Thus every introduction becomes a mini-homily, not an invitation to prayer, and the Eucharist becomes a supreme means of self-expression—for the presider. One of the major reasons that liturgical presidency is problematic today is that it has become so important. If the liturgy stands or falls on the personality of the presider (no matter how "with-it") then all we have accomplished is the exchange of an old form of clericalism for a new form.

This leads to what I call the paradox of liturgical presidency. Presiders cannot "hide" in the new rite; they must be themselves, and they must do this with considerable skill, especially insofar as they affect the whole flow and mood of worship. At one and the same time they must be their genuine, authentic selves and avoid pointing to themselves. Many presiders confuse being their real selves with talking about themselves. Inability to hold authenticity and the rite itself (the possession of the whole assembly) in balance has led to the "star syndrome." As Robert Hovda recently wrote:

> Any practice which communicates the notion that leaders in public worship are "stars" is basically and desperately unproductive, whether the leaders in question are clergy or musicians or any other ministers. Desirable gifts in the leader are no excuse. If her or his style in the particular role fails to communicate a sense of prayerful performance, of *being (first of all) a worshiper and a member of the worshiping assembly,* then he or she is not a leader but an intruder. And the gifts of such a one or such a group damage rather than enhance worship.[38]

To put the matter another way, the most appropriate question that liturgical ministers should ask themselves after a liturgical celebration is not "how did I do?" but rather "did we pray?" If one is looking for stardom, then one should enter the entertainment industry rather than Christian ministry. Genuine human qualities and the prayerfulness of the assembly are best respected when presiders attend to the rite that the community has come to expect (which allows for necessary local adaptations) rather than creating the rite or commenting on it as it goes along.

Contemporary worship indeed suffers from two major difficulties, both related to liturgical presidency. One is the undue appropriation of the rite by presiders or other ministers for their own purposes and the perceived domination of the liturgy by a male celibate clerical establishment. This can be redressed with relative ease: i.e., by ministers respecting the dignity of the assembly and the rite which is the common possession of all. The second difficulty, who can be ordained, is far more complex. Since the very unity of the Church is at stake, the solution is not for local communities to take matters into their own hands, thus potentially causing the kind of split that Walker Percy foresaw in his dark vision of the future.[39] History teaches that schism has never really accomplished lasting good. In an ecumenical era like our own dialogue is far more productive. Short of provoking schism, Roman Catholics must make every effort to force the issue of opening up admission to candidacy for ordination both to women and to married men. Only when that issue is resolved can we get on with the business of our common call—our full vocation to baptismal dignity and to the awesome power of the gospel at work in us and in our liturgical assemblies.

NOTES

1. Walker Percy, *Love in the Ruins: The Adventures of a Bad Catholic at a Time Near the End of the World* (New York: Farrar, Strauss and Giroux, 1971) 5.
2. The necessary nuance would have to explore the tension between chapter 2 of the Constitution on the Church ("The People of God") and chapter 3 ("The Church is Hierarchical"). See Joseph A. Komonchak, "The Local Realization of the Church," in G. Alberigo, J.-P. Jossua, and J. A. Komonchak, eds., *The Reception of Vatican II* (Washington, DC: Catholic University of America Press, 1987) 77–90.
3. See also Luke 22:24-27, where the debate about who is greatest is set within the context of the Last Supper.
4. On this see Karl Rahner, "Considerations on the Active Role of the Person in the Sacramental Event," *Theological Investigations XIV* (Baltimore: Helicon Press, 1976) 169–70.
5. Dogmatic Constitution on the Church 1.
6. *Baptism, Eucharist and Ministry = Faith and Order Paper III* (Geneva: World Council of Churches, 1982) *Eucharist* 29, *Ministry* 23.
7. Edward Schillebeeckx, *The Church With a Human Face: A New and Expanded Theology of Ministry,* trans. John Bowden (New York: Crossroad, 1985) 116.
8. See for example, Hans von Campenhausen, *Ecclesiastical Authority and Spiritual Power in the Church of the First Three Centuries* (Stanford: Stanford University Press, 1969); Raymond Brown, *The Churches the Apostles Left Behind* (New York: Paulist Press, 1984).
9. See Rahner, "Considerations"; also his "On the Theology of Worship," *Theological Investigations XIX* (New York: Crossroad, 1985) 141–49.
10. Bernard Lonergan, *Method in Theology* (New York: Herder & Herder, 1972) 300–302.
11. On the Pauline notion of the body of Christ, see Jerome Murphy-O'Connor, "Eucharist and Community in First Corinthians," in R. K. Seasoltz, ed., *Living Bread, Saving Cup: Essays on the Eucharist,* 2d ed (Collegeville, Minn.: The Liturgical Press, 1987) 1–30. On the changing concept of the body of Christ in the Middle Ages, see the classic treatment by Henri de Lubac, *Corpus Mysticum: Eucharistie et l'Eglise au moyen-age* (Paris: Aubier, 1949).

12. See *Baptism, Eucharist and Ministry: Eucharist* 2–26.

13. See Robert Hovda, "'Priestless Sundays' Reconsidered," *Worship* 62 (1988) 154–59; Gabe Huck, "Why Settle for Communion?" *Commonweal* 37 (1989) 37–39; and especially William Marravee, "'Priestless Masses'—At What Cost?" *Eglise et Théologie* 19 (1988) 207–22. For further bibliography see this last article.

14. Marravee, "Priestless Masses," 220.

15. See Edward Schillebeeckx, *Church*, 256–57; also his *Ministry: Leadership in the Community of Jesus Christ*, trans. John Bowden (New York: Crossroad, 1981) 72–74.

16. On the question of the terminology used of ministers in the New Testament, see Raymond E. Brown, *Priest and Bishop: Biblical Reflections*, (New York: Paulist Press, 1970); Nathan Mitchell, *Mission and Ministry: History and Theology in the Sacrament of Order* (Wilmington, Del.: Michael Glazier, 1982) 107–99; Kenan Osborne, *Priesthood: A History of Ordained Ministry in the Roman Catholic Church* (New York: Paulist Press, 1988) 40–85.

17. See Schillebeeckx, *Church*, 119–20; also Herve-Marie Legrand, "The Presidency of the Eucharist According to the Ancient Tradition," in Seasoltz, *Living Bread*, 197; Paul F. Bradshaw, *Liturgical Presidency in the Early Church* (Bramcote, Nottinghamshire: Grove Books, 1983) 6–8.

18. Joyce Zimmerman, "Priesthood Through the Eyes of a Non-Ordained Priest," *Eglise et Théologie* 19 (1988) 223–29.

19. For example, Elisabeth Schüssler Fiorenza, *In Memory of Her: A Feminist Theological Reconstruction of Christian Origins* (New York: Crossroad, 1983) especially 97–235.

20. See Osborne, *Priesthood*, 30–39.

21. See for example, Edward Kilmartin, *Church, Eucharist and Priesthood* (New York: Paulist Press, 1981) 37–39.

22. Bradshaw, *Liturgical Presidency*, 28.

23. Tertullian, *De exhortatione castitatis* 7:2–6; see Cyrille Vogel, "Is the Presbyteral Ordination of the Celebrant a Condition for the Celebration of the Eucharist?" in A. Triacca, ed., *Roles in the Christian Assembly* (New York: Crossroad, 1981) 253–63.

24. See Schillebeeckx, *Church*, 152.

25. Ibid., 240–44.

26. Peter Brown, *Body and Society: Men, Women, and Sexual Renunciation in Early Christianity* (New York: B. Blackwell, 1988).

27. On the transformation from symbolic to "realist" thinking, see William Crockett, *Eucharist: Symbol of Transformation* (New York: Pueblo Publications Co., 1989) 78ff.; on the medieval relation between Eucharist and priesthood, see Osborne, *Priesthood*, 204ff.

28. *Lumen Gentium* 10; *Presbyterorum Ordinis* 2.

29. On this development see Walter Kasper, "The Priest's Nature and Mission," in his *Faith and the Future* (New York: Crossroad, 1982) 64–85.

30. I do not mean to argue that ordained presbyters might not be associated as liturgical presidents in communities at which they are not full-time pastoral ministers, but it seems to me that they should have some ongoing relation with the assembly.

31. Schillebeeckx, *Church*, 211–34.

32. Joseph Fessio, "Reasons Given Against Women Acolytes and Lectors," *Origins* 17:22 (1987) 399.

33. In A. Flannery, ed., *Vatican Council II: More Postconciliar Documents* (Northport, N.Y.: Costello Publishing Co., 1982) 331–45.

34. On the history of the terminology, see Bernard Marliangeas, *Clés pour une Théologie du Ministère: In Persona Christi, In Persona Ecclesiae* (Paris: Beauchesne, 1978); for recent theological discussion, see David Power, *The Sacrifice We Offer: The Tridentine Dogma and its Reinterpretation* (New York: Crossroad, 1987) 21–26; "Liturgy and Empowerment," in M. A. Cowan, ed., *Alternative Futures for Worship*, Volume 6: *Leadership Ministry in Community* (Collegeville, Minn.: The Liturgical Press, 1987) 81–104; "Sacraments: Symbolizing God's Power in the Church," in *Proceedings of the Catholic Theological Society of America* 1982, 50–66; see also Edward Kilmartin, "Ecclesiastical Office, Power and Spirit," in the same volume, 98–108.

35. For further evaluation of the question of women and ordained ministry, see Leonardo Boff, *Ecclesiogenesis: The Base Communities Reinvent the Church* (Maryknoll, N.Y.: Orbis Books, 1986) 76–97.

36. See Bradshaw, *Liturgical Presidency*, 25–26.

37. Ralph Keifer, *To Give Thanks and Praise* (Washington, D.C.: National Association of Pastoral Musicians, 1980) 97–103.

38. Robert Hovda, "The Amen Corner: Liturgy's Many Roles: Ministers? . . . Or Intruders?" *Worship* 64 (1990) 173.

39. On this issue see my further reflection (with Don Timmerman and Gordon Zahn) in "The Eucharist: Who May Preside?" *Commonweal*, 9 Sept. 1988, 460–66.

Mary Ann Jordan, Psy. D.

Priesthood: Symbol in Crisis

My work as a clinical psychologist brings me in contact with many Catholic lay people and religious who are devoted to prayer, to the Eucharistic liturgy, and to the experience of God as the central reality of human life. I would like to begin this brief essay by sharing an incident which seems to reflect the experience of many American Catholics today.

A sister who was in her seventies came to see me. She explained that each time she participated in the Eucharist, she found herself becoming angry and upset. These emotional reactions deeply disturbed her, for she did not understand their source or cause. She was not a feminist nor was she committed to any special causes. She wanted to come to terms with what was happening to her and to regain her peace of soul.

I recount this vignette because I think this woman's experience is being shared by many other women in the Church today. For some, their anger and frustration are so deep that they have withdrawn from the Eucharist completely. Others no longer participate in the parish celebrations of the Eucharist, preferring instead to gather exclusively with other women who share their pain. Still others are so angry and vocal that dialogue with them often seems virtually impossible to those who do not share their experience. I mention all this because the place and role of women in the Church is a genuinely serious pastoral problem. It is a problem that cannot be ignored, especially when we remember that the Eucharist is the act in which the Church expresses itself and in which the Church's inner unity and its unity with God are experienced and celebrated. So this problem touches what is most fundamental to all of us.

SYMBOLS AND THEIR CULTURAL CONTEXT

I will consider this question from a specific point of view: that of the liturgical presider as a symbol in and for the community. Those of us who are over forty can remember the way Mass was celebrated before Vatican II. We are familiar with the notion of priest as symbol. In those days we could identify with the priest and experience ourselves in union with him as he entered into the mystery of Christ's redemptive act in the celebration of the Mass. The priest's symbolic role beckoned us to enter the mystery of God's presence and love within and among ourselves. Priesthood, as symbol, embodied the transcendent and carried within itself the universality that is essential if symbols are to speak to all persons.

Dramatic changes have occurred in human consciousness and in society which have affected the symbol of priesthood. During the past twenty years we have become conscious of something which has existed unconsciously in our psyches for centuries. We have come to see or to see through the patriarchal conditioning that has affected all of us, women and men, as well as our ancestors, in so many ways. Our new awareness of the degree to which our experience of life and of the world has been shaped by patriarchal views and values, is as momentous, psychologically, as Copernicus's discovery in the sixteenth century that the sun, and not the earth, is the center of the universe. This conditioning is not a feminine problem; it is a human problem that affects us all. A psychological discovery of this magnitude reflects nothing less than a shift in our culture, which means a shift in our understanding of the enculturated symbols through which we experience the Church's message and mission. When such a major cultural shift occurs, as has happened in our day, the symbols of the Church are bound to be affected. The ordained ministry of the Church is a culturally conditioned reality. The symbol that functioned so well before this shift occurred, the male priest as symbol of the holy, is no longer functioning in the same way. The universality of the symbol has been shattered and its inclusiveness has been broken. Many women find themselves upset and disturbed at liturgical celebrations because they experience the symbol of priesthood as exclusive rather than inclusive, as symbolizing patriarchal discrimination rather than access to the holy. The psychological shift has led to a cultural shift which in turn has begun to exert severe pressure on the symbol of liturgical presider.

In saying what it has always said—that only men can be priests—the Catholic Church is now saying something new. Prior to the momentous psychological shift just described, it was possible to regard male priests as symbols because men were the recognized leaders in the public sphere in our culture. As long as that was true, the Church could adequately symbolize "leadership in the realm of the holy" by an all-male priesthood. There was a symbolic "match" between the way the culture understood leadership and male/female relationships and the way the Church understood these things. No one, forty years ago, was seriously saying "I'm a woman and I'd like to be a priest." That just did not occur to us. Today, the culture has changed, in recognition of the fact that women and men are equally competent leaders in the public realm. Faced with this cultural shift, the Church's continued commitment to an all-male priesthood in fact alters the traditional symbolism of ordained ministry. Today, the symbolism of a male priesthood focuses attention on male sexuality, something quite different and new in our tradition. And this is what so many women in the Church today are finding disturbing—that the traditional symbolic content of priesthood (leadership in holiness) has been replaced, by the Church's insistence that only men may be ordained, by a very untraditional content (male sexuality). Those who ask that the Church change its rule to allow the ordination of women are, in fact, appealing to the Church to reassert the traditional content associated with the symbolism of priesthood.

TOWARD WHOLENESS

The patriarchal view of the world has affected all of us. The split which has existed externally in reality throughout the centuries between male and female, men and women, has also been internalized in our psyches. As a result we all experience within ourselves a fundamental conflict between the feminine and the masculine. Those of us who are women have within our psyches repressed, unconscious conflicts that revolve around the masculine. Those of us who are men have within our psyches repressed, unconscious conflicts that revolve around the feminine.

These unconscious conflicts have a bearing on what we feel and experience in the liturgy. An all-male priesthood has come to be an exclusive symbol. As such it taps into and stirs up the inner, painful conflicts and divisions of the psyche. No wonder the liturgy has become for many such an emotion-laden arena. For in the Eucharistic liturgy, with its symbolism of male presidency and priesthood, all these psychological conflicts are focused.

Our task, clearly, is to move beyond the level of conflict to a new level of psychological integration and wholeness. In this task, women have some advantage in having grown up in a Church and in a society where men have traditionally represented the spiritual. Because of this, there may be more of an integration of the masculine within the feminine psyche. Men may well have a more difficult and painful time dealing with this process of integration, for men have rarely (if ever) experienced a woman imaging and representing the divine. The advent of women presiders will touch off much within the male psyche that has been repressed and split off, i.e., the feminine dimension.

From a psychological viewpoint, therefore, this whole question of women's (and men's) leadership roles within the Church is central and pivotal to our lives, not tangential. It has to do with who we are, with our most intimate and personal sense of ourselves as Christians, with our identity as a Church coming together to worship God and enter into the mystery of Christ's redeeming act. In my opinion, there is a psychological inevitability to the ordination of women in the Catholic Church. The inner demands of growth and integration, the demands of psychic wholeness, require it. This is especially so in light of the cultural shifts noted earlier.

We are in transition; we stand at a crossroads. For many of us, it may be a question of "what do we do in the meantime, until that day of psychological wholeness arrives?" Even more to the point, some women today are asking, "why can't we just pick one of ourselves to lead the Eucharist?" Psychologically, I feel this is an inadvisable option, because it threatens to destroy the symbol of leadership just as surely as does our practice of excluding women. As human beings, we all have a need for an ordained presider—a "priest"—who can symbolize our common fund of beliefs and values, our common experience of a God who utterly transcends all our human limitations. We need someone whose function and position within the community is designated and acknowledged by the Church because what that person (whether female or male) carries is the vital link that binds together Christians of all ages in all cultures as the body of Christ. In short, we need someone who can symbolize a reality that transcends all time and all space, for to lose that dimension from the presider is to lose everything, in a way. Authentic symbols integrate and include, they don't separate or exclude. If we are willing to move toward inclusive, growth-producing symbols—symbols whose content points to leadership and the holy, rather than sexual difference—we will have moved much closer to the ineffable mystery and experience of God.

Mary Ann Jordan, Psy. D.

Peter E. Fink, S.J.

Spirituality for Liturgical Presiders

In the years since the Second Vatican Council, the worship experience of Roman Catholics has undergone dramatic changes, not the least of which is expressed concretely in the ministry of the presider. Turning around the altar was not simply a matter of rearranging sanctuary furniture. The stance of the presider, now facing the assembly, signaled a new relationship following from a new consciousness about the meaning of prayer in and through Jesus Christ. It signaled a new awareness of the relationship of presider and assembly. This seemingly simple "rearrangement" prompted a re-examination of the presider's role and the spirituality of those who lead the assembly's prayer.

The ministry of leadership is a central and essential ministry for the assembly gathered to worship. It is a ministry of unity, of welcome, and of prayer, with both existential and symbolic dimensions. Existentially, the call to unity, the welcome, and the prayer must be humanly authentic. Symbolically, these three human ministries present to the assembly the gathering together, the welcome, and the prayer of Jesus Christ. In addition, it is the presider who links the local assembly with both the Church apostolic and the Church universal, thus assuring that the prayer of this local assembly is at one and the same time the prayer of Christ and the prayer of the whole Church. Thus it is that "through the liturgy, especially, the faithful are enabled to express in their lives and manifest to others the mystery of Christ and the real nature of the true Church" (*Sacrosanctum concilium* 2).

CHURCH ORDER

The ministry of presider is assigned variously according to Church order. In Roman Catholic church order, as articulated by the Second Vatican Council, the bishop is the primary presider at the Eucharist, the sacraments of initiation, and the liturgies of ordination. The presbyter, co-worker with the bishop, likewise presides at Eucharist and initiation, as well as all other liturgical actions except ordination. Deacons may be assigned to preside at the liturgies of baptism, marriage, and Christian burial. Lay women and men may preside at services of communion, scripture services, the liturgy of the hours, wake services, and some devotional liturgies. Church order distributes the ministry according to its own rules. The liturgy itself, however, determines both the nature of the ministry and what is required of the presider for the ministry to be properly fulfilled. Thus, what follows applies to the appropriately designated presider, whatever the liturgical gathering.

REQUIREMENTS: SKILLS AND?

The ministry of presider obviously requires specific skills. These include public speaking, poise, the ability to relate to a gathered assembly (indeed, to gather the assembly), artful use of gesture and movement, and, most obviously, knowledge both of the rituals at which one is to preside and of all that is required for their proper and faithful enactment. One must have proper training in these skills. Yet, the ministry of presider involves more than skills. It involves the human and religious truth of the person presiding, and it involves a human and religious journey which the presider must take, both as prerequisite for and as consequence of the ministry which he or she will provide. This human and religious journey is the "stuff" of a spirituality for presiders and the primary focus of these reflections.

My own life and ministry is the principal source of these reflections. I have been presiding at liturgical actions in the Latin Rite for twenty-one years and in the Maronite Rite as well for almost ten. Moreover, at Weston School of Theology I have offered for twelve years the presiding practicum for ordination candidates. In teaching that course, I have tried to give priority to unleashing the potential within these priest-candidates, rather than imposing some uniform pattern of behavior upon them. In addition, in shaping a spirituality for presiders I have been influenced by certain questions from the broader field of sacramental theology, specifically the Vatican II assertion that the priest-presider is one mode of the presence of Christ (SC 7) and the assertion in *Lumen Gentium* that "Though they differ essentially and not only in degree, the common priesthood of the faithful and the ministerial or hierarchical priesthood are none the less ordered one to another; each in its own proper way shares in the one priesthood of Christ" (LG 10).

This paper is not a final statement or a finished product. At the same time, however, it is more than a preamble. It is, perhaps most aptly, "the beginnings of a spirituality for presiders" based upon personal experience and dialogue with others, reflected on and shaped over the years.

A PRELIMINARY CONSIDERATION: KNOWLEDGE OF GOD, KNOWLEDGE OF ONESELF

Before turning to the specific question of a spirituality for presiders, I will offer a more general reflection about the knowledge of God and the knowledge of oneself, and how these two are interwoven in any healthy spirituality. These are not two separate paths of knowing, but rather two distinct objects of knowing revealed along the same path.

Three questions from Scripture help to focus this issue. (1) In the Book of Exodus, God appears to Moses in the desert, giving expression to God's desire to liberate "my people" who are in Egypt, and to send Moses to "bring forth my people, the sons of Israel." Moses puts the first question to God: "Who am I that I should go to Pharaoh, and bring the sons of Israel out of Egypt?" To which God replies simply, "I will be with you" (Exod 3:11-12). (2) Moses then puts a second question to God: "If I come to the people of Israel and say to them, 'The God of your fathers has sent me to you,' and they ask me, 'What is his name?' what shall I say to them?" To which God replies: "JHWH" (Exod 3:13-14), that elusive tetragrammaton which defies translation and which suggests rather than states: "in my own good time I will tell you." (3) The third question is one put by Jesus to his disciples: "Who do you say that I am?" When Peter gives his now famous reply, "You are the Christ, the Son of the living God," Jesus says: "Blessed are you, Simon Bar-Jona! For flesh and blood has not revealed this to you, but my Father who is in heaven" (Matt 16:13-17).

These three questions and the responses given to them unveil a fundamental truth about the knowledge of God. God alone reveals who God is. This revelation comes from God who is present to human life. It is not imposed on human life from the outside; it is spoken and discovered within human life as it is actually lived.

There are, of course, human voices that speak the knowledge of God. Some are noble, some are not. The noble ones arise from the inner faith of others and take shape in the Scriptures, in the journals of the mystics, in the prayers of the liturgy, and in the witness of people who are free enough to speak of the God who is known within them. They are noble because they do not seek to replace God. Rather they speak only to help others meet God themselves; they aim to lead others to the place where God alone will speak. The not-noble voices aim to take the place of God in revealing who God is. They borrow words they do not understand, foist them on others, and seek to get others to do what they think and say God wants (which is really what they want). These not-noble voices are most threatened by the place where God alone will speak.

Here is in fact a handy test of how noble the voices are that speak the knowledge of God. We say that God is gracious, respectful of freedom, always inviting and never coercing. Voices that would speak nobly of God can be no less.

Johannes Metz (in his classic work *Poverty of Spirit*) names the other side of the knowledge of God, focusing on Jesus and at the same time, by reason of the radical nature of the incarnation, on every human person. Metz selects the temptations in the desert, where Jesus was challenged three times, "If you are the Son of God, . . ." According to our strategy, there were two ways for Jesus to determine his true identity: to find it in the voice of the tempter, which is any voice outside of himself, or to listen to the voice of God at his own human core. As Jesus illustrates by his rejoinder, only the second unveils his true human identity. For Jesus, as for every human person, the true human journey is not determined by voices outside, which may also include one's own self-deceptions and illusions, but by going deeper and deeper into one's own human truth.

Metz calls that journey a journey into one's own poverty. Other terms could equally well name it: creaturehood, dependence, nakedness. On that journey where all that clouds our human truth is gradually stripped away, we draw closer to the point where we meet and name both the mystery of God and the mystery of our own true humanity. If we take the incarnation of God with full seriousness, the revelation which God gives to us at that point is not a "voice" we hear, but the person we are; we know God to the extent that we come closer and closer to our own human truth.

Spirituality is the name given to this complex journey, into one's own human truth and into the truth of the mystery of the Holy One. These are not two separate journeys, and they most certainly do not veer in two different directions. Nonetheless, just as there is a Christology from above (with the divinity of Christ as its starting point) and a Christology from below (with the humanity of Christ as its starting point), so there can also be a spirituality from above and a spirituality from below. Different people will lean differently towards one or the other. It does not matter, however, which is given priority in a particular human life; either one necessarily leads along the path of the other as well.

It would seem, then, that since every human life is unique, every spirituality should be unique as well. In one sense this is true, and a healthy spirituality will not seek to reduce the uniqueness of each human life to more general patterns of human behavior. Even so, there is something in the human mystery known as "empathy," the ability of one human person to enter into the life of another and to be at home there. If this were not possible, there would be no such thing as love, and no way in which one person could aid and be aided by the journey of another. Love, ministry, spiritual direction, and guidance all depend on empathy.

This empathy is at the heart of "schools of spirituality" (e.g., Ignatian, Theresian, Pauline, Franciscan) in which the journey of one (Ignatius, Theresa, Paul, Francis) can address, illuminate, and guide the journey of others. Spirituality is never just "your spirituality" versus "my spirituality." In fact empathy is necessary if a true spirituality is to be distinguished from personal illusion. It must be tested. At the same time, empathy, as it is humanly experienced, has a limited range. Not every life is equally successful in guiding the lives of others. To think so is to reduce human uniqueness to an abstraction and to substitute for human life patterns of behavior that can and should be followed by everyone. To the extent, however, that they make sense to others by way of empathy, they gain in currency and value.

These observations, though preliminary, are necessary if one is to address the topic of spirituality for presiders. Spirituality deals in images of God, and the primary images of God which are given to us, as they are named in the Book of Genesis, are men and women and the unique human lives that they lead ("male and female God created them; in God's own image God created them"). The life of each human person is the most privileged image of God he or she will have. All of the other images of

God, be they the poetic images of Scripture, liturgy, and mystical vision or the more abstract images of reflective theology, are subordinate to, and if properly employed illuminative of, the primary image which is each human life. It is commonplace to say that no image of God is identical with God. This must also be said of the uniqueness of each human life. Yet the primacy of human life over all other images must be noted as well. Every man and woman is by creation and by destiny a manifestation, an *imago* of the Holy One. Because of this each person can expect his or her own life to be the primary source of knowledge of the mystery of God.

Of the other images, be they poetic or reflective, three things may be said: (1) they arise from within people's experience, and hence are born within, not outside of, the human journey; (2) they have value to others to the extent that they find an empathic hearing; (3) they are noble if they lead people to God, and they become not-noble when they seek to substitute for God.

A whole range of images of God is given to us in both Scripture and the full Christian tradition of faith and prayer. The psalms, to single out but one book of the Hebrew Scriptures, are replete with them: great benefactor, faithful lover, compassionate caregiver, seeker of justice, playful, vengeful, object of human desire. In the psalms we learn that God is capable of being addressed from almost any human need, yearning, or experience. Some of these images gain our empathy, and are successful in making their appeal to us; others are occasionally of interest; some are repulsive. Some appeal to fear, some to a need for security, some to the affection of love. Nevertheless, none of the images are themselves God, but only ways of identifying God that arise out of the experience of believers, ways by which God invites and leads others along their own journey to both God and their own human truth. The images are spiritually useful if they lead persons to God; they are useless, and possibly dangerous, if they do not.

SPIRITUALITY FOR PRESIDERS

As we turn from this preliminary discussion on the knowledge of God and of oneself, two questions immediately present themselves. Is there such a thing as a spirituality for presiders, and if so in what might it consist?

(a) Is there a specific spirituality for presiders? The question is not a rhetorical one. Three issues urge that it be asked. (1) On the one hand, one observes in the Church today a strong reaction to the centuries-long clerical domination of the liturgy. Phrases like "liturgy is the work of the people," and "liturgy is the action of the whole Church," have captured the popular imagination with force. Any language that would reassert more than a functional role to the presider (whether bishop, priest, deacon, or lay person) is resisted as a threat to return to clerical domination. The question undoubtedly arises: is there a spirituality specific to presiders that does not belong to everyone who participates in the liturgy? My answer is an unequivocal "yes."

(2) On the other hand, there are a number of people within the ranks of the Church who manifest an eagerness to preach and to preside. While this may be a gracious boon, it is not without its difficulties. Many of those who are eager to serve as preacher and presider with enthusiasm and generosity are unaware of the demands of these ministries and their profound challenge. My fear is that such ministers may not bring the proper depth to the task, and when the ministry begins to affect their lives, as it inevitably will, they will not have the resources to recognize, understand, or deal with what is happening.

(3) There is a third issue. It is no secret that there are a number of priests and bishops who by training and temperament "go through the motions," read the texts, do the actions, but never really enter into the ministry which the liturgy and the Church ask of them. They are not good presiders; everyone knows that, but no one knows why. They are not good preachers; everyone knows that, but no one knows why. I suggest that the spirituality of the presider stands at the heart of this problem.

These familiar situations suggest not only the rightness, but also the urgency of addressing the question of a spirituality of liturgical presiders. Thus, the ministry of presider is made all the more important, not less important, because the liturgy is once again recognized as the work of the people and the action of the entire Church. Those who are newly entering this ministry need to know of its costs and of the resources that are available to them to meet those costs. And those who are already serving in this ministry need to be reminded, as *Sacrosanctum concilium* forcefully pointed out, that "when the liturgy is celebrated, something more is required than the laws governing valid and lawful celebration" (SC 11). The quality of preaching and presiding depends upon the spirituality of the presider.

As indicated above, if the ministry of presiding were simply a function, like teaching, facilitating a group, orchestrating a common action, or performing before an audience, there would be no need to explore a specific spirituality. Education and the development of skills would be all that is required. The ministry, however, is not simply a function; it is a presentation of oneself as a person; it taps not simply skills, but the depth of who and what the person is. And as it taps this depth it gives shape and direction to the human and faith journey.

(b) In what does such a spirituality consist? It is helpful to begin with at least a working definition of terms. By the term *spirituality* I mean the integration of one's life of faith within the totality of one's human life. Under "life of faith" comes prayer, one's relationship with God, the claim of grace, the struggle against sin, and the faith, hope, and love inspired by God. "Totality of one's human life" encompasses human affections, sexuality, the struggles proper to an embodied spirit, relationships of all kinds, dreams, aspirations, and desires. The accent is on integration. Two things are thus excluded: (a) locating spirituality in a realm separate from one's human life; and (b) a mythic overlay that overrides one's human struggles and aspirations. Beneath this operational definition lies a conviction that the Holy Spirit of God is an indwelling spirit who is not only wedded to our own deepest desires and aspirations, but is ultimately their source.

Presiders are those who fulfill the specific liturgical ministry which has come to be called, for better or for worse, the "presidency" of the assembly and its liturgical action, whatever that action may be. Current church order distributes this ministry according to certain norms and regulations, requiring ordination for some presidential ministries and not for others; however, the liturgy itself determines what this ministry is. Furthermore, it is the ministry, not the church order, that suggests the appropriate spirituality for those who fulfill the ministry.

The term "president of the assembly" gives little indication as to the content of this ministry or of its spirituality. For this we must turn to the Sacramentary, which is the presider's book. While the

Sacramentary itself is the ritual book for the Eucharistic liturgy, it provides clues for the presider's ministry in all liturgical actions. It is, first of all, a book of prayers, signalling that this ministry is first and foremost a ministry of prayer. (The presider is often called the leader of prayer.)

In addition, the Sacramentary contains directives for greeting, welcome, and invitation, and portrays the presider as one who provides a common focal point, not just for prayer, but also for the many actions that form the heart of the liturgy. The presider thus serves a ministry of unity as well.

The Sacramentary directs that the presider should normally give the homily (different from "proclamation of Scripture", which decidedly does not belong to the presider), in which the word proclaimed and commonly listened to is "opened up" as a living word for "this" assembly. The presiding ministry is a ministry of faith.

If we look beyond the Sacramentary to the liturgical documents that govern it, one final clue as to the nature of this ministry is unveiled: it is a symbolic or iconic ministry captured in the double phrase *in persona Christi* and *in persona ecclesiae*. A key phrase from *Sacrosanctum Concilium* targets this iconic dimension of the presiding ministry: "Christ indeed, always associates the church with himself in this great work in which God is perfectly glorified and men [and women] are sanctified. The church is his beloved bride who calls to her Lord, and through him offers worship to the eternal Father" (SC 7). Note that this double icon or *persona* is not a static reality. It is active toward God in that it embodies the Church "calling out" and "raising up in offering". And it is active toward the people of the Church in that it portrays Christ "gathering" and "associating" the people of the Church in his own worship of *Abba*.

I wish to suggest that the content of a spirituality for presiders is contained in these four elements: (a) ministry of prayer; (b) ministry of unity; (c) ministry of faith spoken to faith; and (d) ministry of being a double icon: of Christ "gathering and associating with himself," and of the Church "calling out" and "offering worship" to *Abba*.

INTEGRATION: JOURNEY OF FAITH, JOURNEY OF LIFE

Each of these four elements of the presiding ministry involves both the humanity and the faith of the minister, but not a faith that is "added onto" humanity or indifferent to it. What is required is the integration of one's life of faith within the totality of one's human life.

The ministry of presider must first of all be humanly true. It taps one's human affections, one's comfort with one's own bodiliness, one's comfort in intimate, sometimes tactile, relationships. It demands that one be humanly vulnerable to the claim of others. The American bishops' *Environment and Art in Catholic Worship* insists that everything in the worship environment should be authentic and true. This is no less true for the presider.

But the ministry of presider is also a religious ministry. The presider is not only "present" to the assembly; the presider is also "present" to the mystery of God. And in this regard as well, one's human affections, one's comfort with one's own bodiliness, one's comfort in intimate, sometimes tactile, relationships comes to bear as one engages the symbols that speak God's presence among us. One must be both humanly and religiously vulnerable to the claim of the mystery of God.

These two realms, the human and religious, are not separate. The human unveils the religious; the religious is expressed through what is human. If we take the incarnation seriously, then one's humanity is a sacrament of the presence of God. Through the person of the presider, Christ's prayer is humanly prayed; Christ's greeting is humanly offered; God's forgiveness is humanly expressed; God's compassion and blessing and care are humanly given. And because this is so, these actions take one on a human journey that is at the same time a journey into God's own mystery.

Two questions help to give shape to a spirituality for presiders: (1) what has to happen to a person if that person will preside at the Church's prayer? and (2) what might happen to a person who in fact does preside at the Church's prayer? The first is an issue of formation: what kind of human journey must the presider take if she or he will fulfill the ministry properly? The second is an issue of consequence, of effect: what kind of human journey will unfold for the presider who fulfills the ministry properly? Both are issues of vulnerability: to the ministry which the Church requests and to the mystery of God who is present in that ministry.

A colleague once asked if the experience of presiding at the Eucharist was any different from the experience of participating as a member of the assembly. I told her it was, but that I wanted some time to reflect on exactly how and why I believed this. What finally came to me is best articulated as "closeness to the symbol set." The symbols of Christian worship express "holy things" and make the Holy One humanly present. Proximity to the symbol set, by touch, gesture, physical locus, and human investment, increases one's vulnerability, both to the "holy things" and to the Holy One. The presiding ministry involves closer proximity to the symbol set of worship than other forms of participating in liturgical action. Negatively, a participant can "tune out" of things without much inner conflict; a presider cannot. Positively, the ministry requires of the presider a level of human investment in the doings that ordinary participation simply does not require.

One can apply the two questions to the four elements of presidential ministry given above. Each of these requires formation before the ministry is undertaken, and each will continue to shape and guide the life of the presider by the very fact that they are carried out.

To lead in prayer requires that the presider learn the ways of prayer and be comfortable in praying publicly. But the prayer of the presiding ministry is not simply one's own personal prayer. The presider prays the prayer of Christ, and thus puts on as his or her own that stance before the Holy One that characterized Jesus' life, and which now constitutes his eternal relationship to *Abba*. To pray thus is to allow oneself and one's own prayer continually to be transformed into that faithful stance. It is to become with Christ "obedient unto death." To be a sign and instrument of unity among people requires in the presider those human characteristics (e.g., reverence for people, compassion and understanding, comfort in the midst of human differences) that invite and summon disparate and sometimes divided people into harmonious relationship. To fulfill that ministry continues to shape the presider in those same characteristics. To speak one's faith requires faith, and the very speaking presents a challenge and summons to believe more firmly. And to be an icon of the Christ who gathers and the Christ who offers requires that the affections of Christ be in some measure appropriated. The very embodiment of those affections that the ministry entails continues to shape one in those same affections.

SPIRITUALITY REFLECTED IN THE RITES

The rituals of ordination for deacon, priest-presbyter, and bishop provide additional insight into the ministry of presiding. Even though the ministry of presider is not, in all cases, restricted to these three groups in the Church, nonetheless, the ordination rites do reveal the Church's expectation and mandate to those whom it commissions to preside, and so by extension to all who preside.

The first point comes from the ordination rite for deacons, when the bishop presents the new deacon with the book of the Gospels: "Receive the Gospel of Christ whose herald you are; believe what you read, preach what you believe, put into practice what you preach." The address to the deacon is more than a pious injunction. It is an exhortation to "make one's own" the gospel one dares to preach. One has no right to preach what one does not believe, nor what has little or no effect in one's life. Both belief and practice are the test of true and authentic preaching.

It is the Church's faith, made clear in our sacramental system, that the gospel of Christ speaks a word of "good news" into human life, and at critical moments as that human life is lived. This points to how and where we discover the truth of our Scriptures. The Vatican II Decree on the Missionary Activity of the Church (*Ad Gentes*) reminds students of theology that it is in the liturgy that they will find the truth of what they study in the classroom (AG 16). It is likewise true that one can discover in one's own human journey the truth of the gospel that is read and preached. Only in facing one's own unbelief can one preach faith; only in facing one's own despair can one preach hope; only in facing one's hatred and/or self-centeredness can one preach love. Only in facing one's experience of death can one preach life after death. Only in facing one's own broken relationships can one preach reconciliation. In one's own human journey one discovers the truth of the gospel that is read and preached, and this journey must be embraced if one is to preach the Word with honesty and integrity.

Furthermore, if one does carry out this ministry and mandate (to believe, preach, and practice), life will more and more take gospel shape, make gospel choices, face gospel struggles. This will necessarily lead the preacher to the One whose fidelity is all Jesus had to rely on. (It is all any of us has to rely on). This is a prime example of the journey into one's own human truth and at the same time a journey into the mystery of God.

Peter E. Fink, S.J.

The second point is taken from the presbyteral ordination rite. The bishop, presenting the bread and wine to the newly ordained, says: "Receive from the people the gifts to be offered to God; know what you are doing, and imitate the mystery that you celebrate." Neither is this a mere pious injunction. It calls the presbyter to understand the full flow of the Eucharistic mystery, and to shape his life according to that mystery.

One of the terms Christian theology uses to express the depth of the Eucharistic mystery is "sacrifice," which focuses on the self-offering of Jesus Christ for the salvation of the world. The sacrificial stance of Christ is eternally *coram Patrem* (towards the Father) in worship and *pro nobis* (for us) as agent of salvation. Christ in his once-for-all sacrifice is made present each time the Eucharist is enacted, and his saving action is presented "under the guise of signs perceptible by the senses" and indeed accomplished "in ways appropriate to each of these signs" (SC 7). To shape one's life according to that sacrificial mystery is to live one's life, and indeed to give one's life, for others in obedience to the summons and desires of God.

When one begins to preside at the Eucharist, one is usually, to be sure, more concerned with knowing the ways of the ritual and enacting it truthfully and faithfully than with issues of spirituality. Nonetheless, the hope is that, just as the new priest has been trained in the ways of the ritual, he has also begun to be formed in a life of obedient worship and generous giving for others. Whether or not this is so, engaging the ritual of Eucharist as presider (where the language and gesture of offering to God for the sake of the many claims both attention and affection), the presider must inevitably be drawn into its sacrificial ways. It is not possible to draw close to the symbols of the mystery without the ways of the mystery playing themselves out in the presider's life. Symbols do not depend on our conscious intent.

The third point is taken from the ordination of bishops where the new bishop is given a twofold admonition: to "listen to the people" and to "model your life after the Shepherd." This is a serious mandate from the Church that will involve the bishop in both the life of Christ and the lives of the people he serves, and by so doing will take him deeply into the mystery of his own human life. The mandate to listen is a mandate to empathy, to being at home in the human journeys of others. It is at the same time a mandate to let others into the bishop's own human journey. The empathy is to be mutual. The mandate to model one's life after Christ is likewise a mandate to mutual empathy, to enter deeply into Christ's human journey, and invite Christ deeply into one's own.

These three points of focus, although articulated in sacramental ritual for the recipients of ordination, name the invitation and challenge to all who would preside at the liturgy of the Church. Presiding is a ministry of proclamation: the word is proclaimed non-verbally as well as verbally in all of life as well as in liturgy. Presiding is a ministry of the worship of God and a ministry of Christ's saving action toward people. And presiding is a ministry of relationship to Christ and to the assembly which involves "being Christ in icon" and listening to the people with Christ's own attentiveness. In liturgical actions Christ, our one high priest, "always associates the Church with himself in this great work in which God is perfectly glorified and men [and women] are sanctified" (SC 7). Existentially and symbolically the presider serves that association.

CONCLUSION

The ministry of presider is not a disembodied function. It is a human ministry that calls on one's full humanity to unveil and to serve the mystery of God. In turn it makes human life vulnerable to the mystery that is served. It demands that the presider take on the desires and the affections of God, the desires and affections of Christ, and the hopes and aspirations of a sinful and holy Church in a sinful and grace-filled world. One does not take on this ministry lightly. It demands much even before the presider begins; it continues to demand much as the symbols with which the presider is engaged shape and guide the presider's own life. They will take the presider into the mystery they express; the mystery in turn will unfold in the presider's life. And sooner or later the presider will be drawn to where Jesus himself was drawn: to the One who is addressed in prayer, the One whom Jesus names *Abba*, the One whose constant fidelity to the human journey Jesus himself reveals. And that place of meeting will be as it was for Jesus himself at the core of the presider's own human truth. For there, at the "dregs of poverty," to use Metz's phrase, is worship.

Peter E. Fink, S.J.

John R. Page

ICEL Through Twenty-five Years

INTRODUCTORY REMARKS

Everyone likes a birthday surprise. ICEL is no exception. Last October (1988) ICEL celebrated its twenty-fifth anniversary. It was soon after that that I received a call from the Notre Dame Center for Pastoral Liturgy informing me that ICEL had been chosen as the 1989 recipient of the Michael Mathis Award. This was easily the best birthday present ICEL received, and I wasted no time in letting the bishops and advisors of ICEL's farflung world know this good news. The reaction was delight and gratitude. I cannot say that all these people knew of Father Mathis and his contributions, but all of them certainly knew the great name of Notre Dame, its academic programs and pastoral center, its many accomplishments in the area of liturgical scholarship and renewal. The contributions of Notre Dame in this regard are admired all over the English-speaking world.

ICEL itself owes a great debt to Notre Dame's liturgical program, its faculty and graduates, and to the Center for Pastoral Liturgy, its staff and programs. The list of Notre Dame people who have participated in and fostered ICEL's task is a very long one and this participation extends through every phase of ICEL's work.

It would be good on an occasion like this to claim some direct connection with Michael Mathis either by way of acquaintance or inspiration. I can claim neither. In an effort to remedy this defect as best I could, I made a pilgrimage last night after evening prayer to Father Mathis's grave here on the campus. There I said a prayer of gratitude for his work and that of the other liturgical pioneers. They sowed, we reap. I like to think that Michael Mathis's role in the American ritual of 1954 would have given him a great deal of sympathy and respect for the problems and challenges faced by ICEL, particularly in the area of liturgical translation.

In what follows I will tell the story of ICEL, why we have it, how it works—a congenial task for a historian who has strayed to other fields. To tell the story of ICEL is to tell again in part the story of the Second Vatican Council.

We may well be scandalized by Browning's Renaissance bishop spending his dying breath ordering in careful detail his tomb at St. Praxed's Church in Rome, especially when he contemplates the prospect of how he shall "lie through centuries/And hear the blessed mutter of the mass." But those who knew the Mass twenty-five years ago might not be altogether surprised to hear a man of the bishop's cynical faith describe the celebration of the Eucharist in that way.

On 11 October 1962 as the Fathers of the Second Vatican Council walked in uneven ranks across St. Peter's Square towards the basilica and the opening of the council, few if any of them were likely to have had large expectations for the liturgy in the vernacular as they thought of the historic occasion in which they were about to participate. Ahead of them that day they faced a liturgy four hours long, almost totally in Latin, broken only by the chanting (as was the custom at Papal Masses) of the epistle and gospel in Greek. Through each of the four sessions to come they would listen for several hours every day to speeches in Latin. With teams of Latinists assembled in Rome, none of the bishops seemed dismayed by this latter prospect, at least not publicly, except for Cardinal Cushing (who went home) and the Melchite Patriarch who stayed and spoke in French. Latin held its place in the Roman Church and despite some hopes for limited use of the vernacular in the liturgy, the possibility of a liturgy totally in English seemed very far away, if not impossible. The Roman Church was practically synonymous with the Latin liturgy, and Latin was held up as one of the most important factors in preserving the Church's unity. In February 1962, just eight months before the council opened, Pope John XXIII in the apostolic constitution *Veterum sapientia* upheld the place of Latin in the Church and decreed its use by professors in seminaries throughout the Latin Church. Indeed a special institute was to be set up in Rome to foster study of the Latin language in the Church and to ensure that seminaries and chanceries all over the world would have on hand priests who were expert in Latin. On the use of Latin in the liturgy *Veterum sapientia* had this to say: "The Catholic Church has a dignity far surpassing that of every merely human society, for it was founded by Christ the Lord. It is altogether fitting, therefore, that the language it uses should be noble, majestic, and non-vernacular."

Debates over the use of modern languages in the Church's worship go back through several centuries to the heretical movements of the high Middle Ages, to Trent in the sixteenth century, the Chinese Rites controversy in the seventeenth, the Synod of Pistoia in the eighteenth, and to Joseph Berington and John Lingard in England early in the nineteenth century. But until the twentieth century the debate was largely isolated and ineffective. It is interesting to recall that it was only under Pope Leo XIII at the end of the nineteenth century that translations of the Roman Missal were allowed to be published in hand missals intended for lay people.[1]

It is not necessary here to recount the development of the liturgical movement in this century. But certainly one aspect of it was a concern on the part of some of its leaders to make more of the liturgy available in the vernacular. The charter of the modern liturgical movement was, of course, Pope Pius XII's encyclical *Mediator Dei* (20 November 1947). Paragraph 60 of that encyclical states that "the use of the Latin language prevailing in a great part of the Church affords at once an imposing sign of unity and an effective safeguard against the corruption of true doctrine. Admittedly the adoption of the vernacular in quite a number of functions may prove of great benefit to the faithful. But the Apostolic See alone is empowered to grant this permission." And so there was for the first time a foot in the door, and within little more than twenty years the door would be wide open.

In the 1950s the Holy See allowed national hierarchies the limited use of the vernacular in the Ritual. English, though in a restricted way, began to be used in such rites as baptism, marriage, anointing of the sick. Each individual hierarchy was responsible for overseeing the rituals that contained some parts in the vernacular. There was no effort made to ensure common texts for countries using the same language. Father Michael Mathis was largely responsible for directing the preparation of the English version of the *Collectio Rituum*, published in the United States in 1954.[2]

The situation at the opening of the council did not give much encouragement to promoters of a full vernacular liturgy. There were, to be sure, groups calling for a total vernacular liturgy.[3] Many countries had their vernacular societies, but these were often looked on with suspicion, and it was shortly before the Council that a leading American liturgist was kept from teaching summer school at a major Catholic university because of his radical views, especially his proposals for the use of the vernacular in the liturgy.

The Council's debates on the schema on the liturgy began on 22 October 1962. The schema itself introduced the possibility of some use of the vernacular in the Mass and sacraments.[4] It became quickly apparent that there were a number of bishops, especially from northern Europe but also from other areas, who were in favor of a greatly increased use of the vernacular. These bishops were often careful to speak of the pride of place to be given to the Latin and were not advocates of a total replacement of Latin. Certainly there were also voices raised in opposition to any use of the vernacular, and there was also a group of bishops who were willing to concede a wider use of the vernacular in the administration of the sacraments and sacramentals but were totally against its use in the Mass, with the possible exception of the readings.[5] All of those who spoke in favor of some use of the vernacular, whether limited or broad, advanced pastoral concerns as their reasons for proposing such changes. In the end it was this pastoral concern which would inform the whole Constitution on the Liturgy and which would open the way, though not fully, to the situation we have today.

Let us look briefly at some of the key passages with respect to the vernacular in the Constitution on the Liturgy. An important statement comes early in the constitution: "In this reform both texts and rites should be so drawn up that they express more clearly the holy things they signify and that the Christian people, as far as possible, are able to understand them with ease and to take part in the rites fully, actively, and as befits a community" (*Sacrosanctum Concilium* 21).[6] Here the broad principle is set forth without mentioning the vernacular as such. This will come a few paragraphs later in article 36. Significantly, article 36 begins by stating that "the use of the Latin language is to be preserved in the Latin rite." That said, however, the historic moment immediately follows:

> But since the use of the mother tongue, whether in the Mass, the administration of the sacraments, or other parts of the liturgy, frequently may be of great advantage to the people, the limits of its use may be extended. This will apply in the first place to the read-

ings and instructions and to some prayers and chants, according to the regulations on this matter laid down for each case.

And, important for my purpose here, the third part of article 36 goes on to say that decisions regarding the use of the vernacular will be, following the norms of the Holy See, under the authority of the local hierarchies.[7]

Articles 54 and 63 of the Constitution on the Liturgy spelled out in greater detail that the use of the vernacular was to be allowed not only for the Mass but also for the sacraments[8] and though the constitution speaks primarily of the readings and the prayer of the faithful in the vernacular and also of the possibility of the parts belonging to the people being in the vernacular, it also goes on to speak in article 54 of further possibilities by stating that "whenever a more extended use of the mother tongue within the Mass appears desirable," this must be carefully thought out beforehand by the local conference and submitted to the judgment of the Apostolic See. The Constitution on the Liturgy had then on the face of it taken a middle course—pride of place to the Latin, the sacraments and some parts of the Mass in the vernacular, and an opening towards "a more extended use of the mother tongue within the Mass." By the time the Constitution was promulgated on 4 December 1963 a veritable sea-change had occurred in the Roman Church's sixteen-century-old adherence to Latin as the language of the liturgy. Within just a few short years the possibility of a "more extended use" would in fact lead to the whole of the Church's liturgy being in the vernacular.

RAPID DEVELOPMENT

Amazingly, within the brief period from the approval of the Constitution on the Liturgy in December 1963 through early 1967 the possibility of the whole liturgy in the vernacular, including the Mass, was achieved. The first concessions, as outlined in *Inter Oecumenici*,[9] following the constitution, spoke of allowing the vernacular for the readings, the prayer of the faithful, the chants and antiphons, recited or sung parts such as the Gloria, the Creed, the acclamations, greetings, and the Lord's Prayer. Further extensions of the vernacular in the Mass were given in 1965 and 1966. In January 1967 Pope Paul VI allowed, at first *ad experimentum*, the use of the vernacular in the canon of the Mass and in the rites of ordination. The progress from limited concessions to the full liturgy in the vernacular can be followed in part through the series of documents from the Pope and the Consilium for the Implementation of the Constitution on the Liturgy in the period between 1964 and 1967, but undoubtedly a good part of the story was carried out behind the scenes.[10] No doubt also, the numerous requests received by the Holy See from individual hierarchies asking for concessions of the vernacular beyond those envisaged in the constitution had a major part in this sudden shift.[11] It is interesting to speculate on the effect that the concession granted for the recitation of the divine office in the vernacular may have had on opening up the possibilities for a fully vernacular liturgy. First conceded in article 101 of the constitution "to those clerics for whom the use of Latin constitutes a grave obstacle to their praying the office properly," this concession was reconfirmed in 1964 in *Sacram Liturgiam* and in *Inter Oecumenici*.[12] It is well known that within the space of two or three years most of those bound to the recitation of the office had taken advantage of this concession, and no doubt the anomaly soon became apparent: if people who knew some Latin found it difficult to pray the office, people who knew no Latin could surely be expected to have difficulty praying the Mass.

There must soon have come a realization that retaining Latin for the Liturgy of the Eucharist made the Liturgy of the Word seem a secondary element, "a period of instruction to be followed by a sacred action preserved in an ancient tongue,"[13] and, as a consequence, the intent of the whole conciliar reform of the Mass would have been thrown askew. While this realization also undoubtedly had a place in the shift that took place, there can be no doubt that the major impetus for the rapid change to the full vernacular was the pastoral sense of the bishops, intensified by the Council experience and now being put into practical effect in their local areas. And certainly the role of Pope Paul VI cannot be underestimated. Reading his various talks on implementing the reform, given at general audiences in the several years just after 1963, one gets the sense of how acutely he felt the loss of the Latin, but how firmly he felt that the vernacular must replace it if the reform envisioned by the Council was to take root.

The years just after the promulgation of the Constitution on the Liturgy also saw important developments in the understanding of mixed or joint commissions of bishops' conferences working together to produce uniform texts for those speaking the same language. From the constitution's article 36, which said that bishops of nearby territories of the same language should consult together before preparing vernacular translations, we move to Cardinal Lercaro, who, in his capacity as President of the Consilium, wrote on 16 October 1964 to the presidents of the conferences of bishops that

> The Consilium accordingly wishes to make known its mind on the special issue of vernacular versions in regions using the same language: in these regions uniformity is to be maintained in the texts for vernacular celebration of the liturgy. Approval of multiple versions, texts, and editions in one and the same language, especially in such major languages as English, French, German, and Spanish, seems ill-advised; it would be detrimental both to the importance of the texts themselves and to the dignity of the liturgical books.[14]

Cardinal Lercaro's endorsement of mixed commissions was confirmed by Pope Paul VI in his allocution to translators of liturgical texts on 10 November 1965.[15] International mixed commissions were endorsed further in the opening paragraph of the "Instruction on the Translation of Liturgical Texts," issued on 25 January 1969.[16]

THE BIRTH OF THE INTERNATIONAL COMMISSION ON ENGLISH IN THE LITURGY AND ITS MANDATE

The International Commission on English in the Liturgy was founded at the very heart of the Council. It began prosaically enough when several bishops from English-speaking countries gathered in a restaurant in Rome in the autumn of 1962, just after the opening of the Council. Most likely these bishops had no strong expectations that the whole of the liturgy would be allowed in the vernacular, nor did they necessarily think clearly of having one common text for use wherever English was spoken. But they saw at least some advantages to sharing the many resources available to the Church in the English-speaking countries and they perhaps already foresaw, as they would certainly foresee by the next year, the significant help that the larger English-speaking countries could provide to the smaller countries. This first informal meeting of what was to become ICEL was called by Archbishop Paul Hallinan of Atlanta, who was the only American to serve on the council's Commission on the Liturgy. Those present at the meeting spoke to others from their conferences during the first session of the council and gradually, as article 36 was debated, a plan was formed to convene a formal meeting early in the second session of the Council with representatives of all the conferences where English was the primary or a major secondary language. By this stage it had become apparent to Archbishops Hallinan, Denis Hurley of Durban, South Africa, Francis Grimshaw of Birmingham, England, and Guilford Young of Hobart, Australia, that a common translation for all English-speaking countries might be possible and even desirable. In the spring of 1963 Archbishop Hurley took the initiative of drawing up a detailed plan to be discussed by the representatives of the hierarchies at the meeting proposed for later in the year.[17]

The first formal meeting was convened in Rome at the English College on 17 October 1963. Representatives of ten conferences were present: Australia, Canada, England and Wales, India, Ireland, New Zealand, Pakistan, Scotland, South Africa, and the United States. (In 1967 the Philippines would become the eleventh member conference.) At this first meeting the bishops recognized the need to create a body of scholars who would carry out the work of preparing the English liturgical texts. This was the beginning of ICEL's advisory committee and it was to this body, then called the International Advisory Committee on English in the Liturgy, that the bishop representatives of the ten conferences meeting again in Rome in October 1964 addressed a mandate, the principal charges of which were:

1. To work out a plan for the translation of liturgical texts and the provision of original texts where required, in language which would be correct, dignified, intelligible, and suitable for public recitation and singing;

2. to propose the engagement of experts in various fields as translators, composers, and critics and to provide for the exchange of information with the sponsoring Hierarchies and with other interested Hierarchies; and

3. to give special attention, within the scope of this plan, to the question of a single English version of the Bible for liturgical use or at least of common translations of biblical texts used in the liturgy.[18]

In time the bishops, with one representative from each of the member conferences, came to be known as the episcopal board.

The specialists were designated as simply the Advisory Committee. Both groups were then included under the overall designation "The International Commission on English in the Liturgy" or ICEL.

Though a number of external translators and consultants were involved in the work from the earliest years, the advisory committee at times had to function also as a translating committee. By the mid-1970s the structure had been somewhat altered by the establishment of standing subcommittees to work under the advisory committee. This allowed the advisory committee to have the role of a central steering body for programs and policies, subject always to the ratification of the board of bishops. At the present time there are subcommittees on translations and revisions, original texts, the presentation of texts, music, and a liturgical psalter. The subcommittees are made up of specialists in the particular field or fields of the subcommittee's work. Though two or three members of the advisory committee sit on each subcommittee, the majority of the membership comes from outside that body. This system ensures a broader participation in the work by scholars from different parts of the English-speaking world. To coordinate the day-to-day work of ICEL, a secretariat was established in Washington in 1965.

The process ICEL has followed from the first in the preparation and presentation of its work can be briefly summarized as follows: one person (in some cases two or three people) prepares a draft text. This is then reviewed by the full subcommittee. If the subcommittee approves the text, it is then presented to the advisory committee. With the approval of the advisory committee, this text then becomes the provisional or draft version or, in ICEL's special argot, the "Green Book." It is then submitted to all of the bishops of the English-speaking world and to their consultants for study and comment. Often a conference of bishops will decide for various reasons to approve the use of the draft text in the liturgy for an interim period until the final text is ready. (Such was the case in the United States with the *Dedication of a Church and An Altar* and the *Book of Blessings.*) When the period for comments on the use of the draft text is over, the subcommittee on translations reviews all comments received, and in light of them begins to prepare the "White Book" or final text. After this, the text goes again to the advisory committee. If the advisory committee approves, the text is submitted to the episcopal board. The episcopal board must approve a final ICEL text by a two-thirds majority. If this is reached, the text is then presented to the eleven member and fifteen associate-member conferences of bishops. It is up to each conference of bishops to decide whether or not to use the ICEL text. To be approved a text must gain a two-thirds majority vote of the members of an individual conference. With that vote the text is then sent to the Holy See for the required confirmation. When the confirmation has been received, the individual conference promulgates the text as the official version for use in that conference.

In 1967 the first ICEL text, the Roman Canon (Eucharistic Prayer I), was presented to the conferences of bishops. Between 1967 and 1989, when the *Ceremonial for Bishops* was completed, ICEL prepared some thirty separate and distinct liturgical books, including such vast undertakings as the Roman Missal and The Liturgy of the Hours, and issued another seventy or eighty supplementary documents and commentaries, including the fifteen-hundred page *Documents on the Liturgy,* published in 1983, and several books of musical settings for the rites: baptisms, funerals, ordinations.

Twenty years may seem a long time in a lifetime, but it is a short period in the Roman Church's present development of vernacular liturgies, particularly when measured against the long centuries of Latin. A great deal has been accomplished in the past two decades. There have been interim translations of interim books, interim translations of revised books, final translations of revised books. And now ICEL has begun a new phase: a further revision of the revised books. From ICEL's earliest years a time of revision had been foreseen. Indeed the Holy See's 1969 "Instruction on the Translation of Liturgical Texts," a major document in steering the Church's transition from the Latin to the vernacular liturgy, looked forward to the need periodically to revise texts in living languages.[19] The first years of ICEL had an enthusiasm that looked towards having the English texts as soon as possible. Bishops, priests, and laity were anxious, even impatient, to have the texts. Once the process started it moved at nearly breakneck speed as effective dates for the use of the newly revised rites succeeded one another. The original members of ICEL's advisory committee certainly knew that their work would have to be reviewed again in a calmer time, after the first excitement and sense of urgency had died down. And the members of the episcopal board reminded their conferences in those years that revisions would eventually be needed.

THE WORK OF REVISION

In the late 1970s, with a major part of ICEL's translation program accomplished, the episcopal board announced that ICEL would in the next several years begin a comprehensive program of revisions. The intent of this program was to refine and revise the texts, some of which by the time the program was launched would have been in use for a decade or more. It was felt that by the time the revisions program began, a sufficient period would have elapsed for a considered reaction to the texts from all segments of the praying Church. This program also looked towards the provision of new or originally composed texts which, with the exception of the alternative opening prayers of the Sacramentary and some other brief texts in the Order of Mass, had been impossible to prepare in the years when ICEL was faced with a very heavy program of translation. It was decided that a consultation to be carried out as widely as possible would be held for each separate rite. Special consultation books would be prepared and distributed at each stage. The whole process was expected to last from ten to fifteen years.

The first consultation book—on the revision of the *Rite of Funerals*—was issued in February 1981. The *Rite of Funerals* was chosen as the first step because it was one of the earliest texts prepared by ICEL and, since it is a fairly brief rite, it allowed for a controlled, limited beginning to the revisions program.[20] It was hoped that this limited beginning would show the best method for proceeding with subsequent stages of the program, especially since in time revisions of very large groups of texts, such as the Roman Missal and The Liturgy of the Hours, would have to be undertaken.

The period of revision gives ICEL the opportunity to go further in two important respects: the provision of original prayers and the pastoral presentation of the contents of the liturgical books.[21]

ORIGINAL TEXTS

From the beginning, ICEL saw the need for original texts. This was incorporated into the mandate given by the founding bishops to the first committee of specialists in 1964. The 1969 "Instruction on the Translation of Liturgical Texts" also saw unambiguously the need for original texts. The concluding paragraph (no. 43) of that document states that "texts translated from another language are clearly not sufficient for the celebration of a fully renewed liturgy. The creation of new texts will be necessary. But translation of texts transmitted through the tradition of the Church is the best school and discipline for new texts so that any new forms adopted should in some way grow organically from forms already in existence."[22]

In the revisions process ICEL is devoting a good deal of its energies towards providing newly composed texts. This in itself is an ambitious project. For example, in the revision of the Missal now under way, over three hundred new texts are planned, including opening prayers for Sundays and solemnities related to the Scripture readings of the day. The composition of new texts is very difficult work and ICEL's experience has taught it that the creation of original liturgical texts is a rare talent. But if ICEL can succeed in this effort our body of prayer texts will be greatly enriched in an idiom and imagery completely native to English.

In the first of the revised books, the *Order of Christian Funerals*, issued to the conferences of bishops in 1985, forty new or original texts were provided, such as prayer for a stillborn child, prayers for one who died by suicide, and prayers for use at the funeral of an elderly person.

The following text is one of two original prayers provided for the difficult pastoral situation when death is the result of suicide:

> God, lover of souls
> you hold dear what you have made
> and spare all things, for they are yours.
> Look gently on your servant N.,
> and by the blood of the cross
> forgive his/her sins and failings.
>
> Remember the faith of those who mourn
> and satisfy their longing for that day
> when all will be made new again
> in Christ, our risen Lord,
> who lives and reigns with you for ever and ever.
> R. Amen.[23]

One of the new prayers for a baptized child reads:

Lord God,
source and destiny of our lives,
in your loving providence
you gave us N.
to grow in wisdom, age, and grace.
Now you have called him/her to yourself.

As we grieve over the loss of one so young
we seek to understand your purpose.[24]

Draw him/her to yourself
and give him/her full stature in Christ.
May he/she stand with all the angels and saints,
who know your love and praise your saving will.

We ask this through Christ, our Lord.

R. Amen

A comment on each of these prayers will illustrate, very briefly, some of the thought that went into their composition. Death by suicide is clearly a painful tragedy that demands great pastoral sensitivity and delicacy. Not so many years ago the Church approached the situation very restrictively. While considerable pastoral discretion is still called for, the possibility for celebrating the Church's funeral rites publicly for someone who has committed suicide is now far more open. The example given here takes its inspiration from Wisdom 11–12, and to a lesser extent from Gerard Manley Hopkins's "In the Valley of the Elwy."[25] The passage from Wisdom is the powerful section which reads:

For you love all things that are
  and loathe nothing that you have made;
  for what you hated, you would not have fashioned.
And how could a thing remain, unless you willed it;
  or be preserved, had it not been called forth by you?
But you spare all things, because they
  are yours, O Lord and lover of souls,
  for your imperishable spirit is in all things!

Wisdom 11:24–12:1 (New American Bible)

The first section of the prayer speaks of the love and compassion of God for all creation; God cannot hate what he has made. It moves then to ask for forgiveness and mercy, taking up an echo from the Hopkins poem, "Complete thy creature dear O where it fails." The second section of the prayer is a strong faith-filled plea, made trustingly in the promise of Jesus' resurrection, both for the mourners and the one who has died.

The prayer for a baptized child attempts to speak realistically about the situation that the parents, brothers and sisters, relatives and friends of the child are experiencing. This is particularly true of the middle section of the prayer. Yet overall there is a sense of hope and confidence in God's care. The ending lines speak strongly of a new life in the company of all who have struggled to believe and do God's will throughout the ages.

PRESENTATION

The presentation of the contents has to do with making the book a useful pastoral instrument. A lot of this concerns the design and format of each page. But it is more than this. In the *Order of Christian Funerals* a new twelve-page introduction, more suited to pastoral situations in English-speaking countries, has been provided along with the Roman introduction. The new General Introduction explains the rearrangement of the rites and provides a more developed pastoral theology for celebrating funerals and ministering to the bereaved. It gives a broader view of the ministry of the community in the funeral rites and develops in detail the principle given in paragraph 9 of the new introduction that "the responsibility for the ministry of consolation rests with the believing community." This principle is spelled out throughout the general introduction and particular introductions to each section of the book, and strong emphasis is given to the community's presence and participation in the celebration of the funeral rites. More attention is given to liturgical elements (music, psalmody, readings), to the role of the liturgical ministers (readers, musicians, ushers, pallbearers), and to the overall environment for worship.

Far more material, for example, has been added for the funeral rites of children, including a "Rite of Final Commendation for an Infant" that can also be used in a hospital as a brief rite following a stillbirth. And, by way of further example, brief model rites have been provided for use with the family gathered immediately after the death of a relative or for a first gathering of family members in the presence of the body prepared for burial.

The clarifying notes and rubrics have been added to the text not to regiment and regulate but to suggest and invite in a prayerful, meditative way the minister's preparation against the background of the Church's theology of death and how that is enunciated in the liturgical rites for the death and burial of a baptized Christian.

Unfortunately, there is no time to say more than a word about the revision of the Roman Missal (Sacramentary), begun several years ago and now past the halfway mark as ICEL looks towards presenting the revised text to the conferences in 1993. It is, I think, a landmark undertaking in the history of English liturgical prayer. An eighty page "Progress Report," with examples, on the revision of the texts translated from the Latin was issued to the bishops last year. Three other progress reports on the other phases of the revision will be issued over the next year and a half.

CONCLUSION

The expectations for the vernacular on the eve of the council were limited. Within very few years, we moved from these circumscribed hopes to a liturgy totally in English. Only four years after the opening of the council we hear Pope Paul VI saying in his defense of Cardinal Lercaro:

> Latin is an issue certainly deserving serious attention, but the issues cannot be solved in a way that is opposed to the great principle confirmed by the Council, namely, that liturgical prayer, accommodated to the understanding of the people, is to be intelligible. Nor can it be solved in opposition to another principle called for by the collectivity of human culture, namely, that peoples' deepest and sincerest sentiments can best be expressed through the vernacular as it is in actual usage.[26]

In 1969 the same Pope said at a general audience: "Our understanding of prayer is worth more than the previous, ancient garments in which it has been regally clad. Of more value, too, is the participation of the people, of modern people who are surrounded by clear, intelligible language. . . ."[27]

We can hope that at the Church of Santa Prassede, Browning's bishop, in the splendor of his Renaissance tomb, may lie less easily for what has been done over the past twenty-five years. And there is still much to be done. May the Lord guide our steps.

NOTES

1. That this sanction was frequently ignored is amply demonstrated by J. D. Crichton in *Worship In a Hidden Church* (Dublin: The Columbia Press, 1988). On English translations of texts from the *Missale Romanum* before the lifting of the Roman prohibition, see also Joseph P. Chinnici, O.F.M., *The English Catholic Enlightenment: John Lingard and the Cisalpine Movement 1780–1850* (Shepherdstown: The Patmos Press, 1980).
2. Knowledgeable observers believe that the draft version of *Veterum sapientia* suppressed the vernacular rituals sanctioned just eight years previously. The final version, however, contained no such prohibition.
3. Participants at the Assisi Congress in 1956 had been disappointed when Pius XII, in the talk he gave to the participants at the concluding session in Rome, failed to mention the use of the vernacular in the liturgy.
4. Archbishop Denis Hurley, a member of the Central Preparatory Commission that was convened by Rome to prepare for the Council, recalls his growing discouragement as each draft schema was presented to the bishops during their periodic meetings in Rome from 1960 to 1962. On one of the long journeys between South Africa and Rome he took from his briefcase the latest schema that had been presented to the preparatory commission. It was the draft of the schema on the liturgy and suddenly his whole attention was absorbed in its contents. For the first time he had hope for the success of the Council. The schema on the liturgy was the only preparatory draft to survive the scrutiny of the bishops assembled for the Council.
5. The varieties of opinion are probably best and curiously illustrated by a prominent American archbishop who was fully in favor of the use of the vernacular in the breviary but against its use in the Mass.
6. Vatican Council II, Constitution on the Liturgy (*Sacrosanctum Concilium*), 4 December 1963, art. 21: ICEL, *Documents on the Liturgy, 1963–1979: Conciliar, Papal, and Curial Texts* (hereafter, DOL) (Collegeville, Minn.: The Liturgical Press, 1982) 1, no. 21.
7. The authority given to conferences of bishops for the liturgy is first mentioned in article 22 of *Sacrosanctum Concilium* but the reference in 36, 3 is its first practical enunciation. In this respect the Constitution on the Liturgy clearly anticipated *Christus Dominus,* which was promulgated two years later.
8. A last-minute attempt to mandate the retention of the sacramental form in Latin was defeated by the Fathers of the council. The documents implementing the liturgical reform did, however, take a very restrictive position on the use of the vernacular in the ordination rites. This restriction was removed by Pope Paul VI in January 1967 at the same time as the restriction against the use of the vernacular for the Eucharistic Prayer (Roman Canon) was removed. But even here an exception was made for the sacramental forms of the ordination rites. The decision as to whether they too

should be translated into the vernacular was left to the conferences of bishops. This limitation was withdrawn several months later. See DOL 117, no. 816 (31 January 1967) and DOL 39, no. 474 (4 May 1967).

9. DOL 23, nos. 349–52 (26 September 1964).

10. The Consilium, the body which was to have the leading role in the implementation of the conciliar reform of the liturgy, was inaugurated on 5 March 1964. Its role in the extension of the vernacular beyond the conciliar enactments cannot be directly shown, but there can be no doubt that the majority of the members and consultors favored such extensions. The whole thrust of their work made this evident. Consequently the influence of the Consilium on the move to a full vernacular use must be acknowledged. It is appropriate to note here that six of ICEL's founders were named to the Consilium as members or consultors. They were Archbishops Paul Hallinan of Atlanta, United States, Denis Hurley of Durban, South Africa, Guilford Young of Hobart, Australia, Francis Grimshaw of Birmingham, England, and the two American *periti,* Fathers Godfrey Diekmann, O.S.B. of St. John's Abbey, Collegeville, and Frederick McManus of the Catholic University of America.

11. A good account of the U.S. conference of bishops' gradual extension of the vernacular in the Mass from 1965 to 1967 is given in Thomas J. Shelley, *Paul J. Hallinan* (Wilmington, Del.: Michael Glazier, 1989) 239–58. Archbishop Hallinan, along with Archbishop John Dearden of Detroit, played a leading role in these developments. See also Frederick R. McManus (ed.), *Thirty Years of Liturgical Renewal* (Washington, D.C.: The Office of Publishing and Promotion Services, National Conference of Catholic Bishops, 1987).

12. DOL 20, no. 287 (25 January 1964) and DOL 23, nos. 86–89 (26 September 1964).

13. Mark Searle, "Reflections on Liturgical Reform," *Worship* 56 (September 1982) 418.

14. DOL 108, no. 764.

15. DOL 113, no. 788.

16. DOL 123, nos. 878–79.

17. See Frederick R. McManus, *ICEL: The First Years* (ICEL: Washington, D.C., 1981) 5–6.

18. See McManus, *ICEL: The First Years,* 12–13.

19. DOL 123, no. 838.

20. In the revisions process the published text that has been in use for ten or fifteen years takes the place in a sense that the "Green Book," the draft text issued for study and comment, had in the initial phase of preparing the liturgical books in English.

21. Though it does not fall, strictly speaking, in the series of ICEL's revised books, *Pastoral Care of the Sick: Rites of Anointing and Viaticum,* issued in

1982, is also a notable example of ICEL's new effort to provide fuller, richer liturgical books for use in the English-speaking conferences.

22. DOL 123, no. 880.

23. This text replaces another prayer for a person who committed suicide that appeared in the *Order of Christian Funerals* as presented by ICEL to the conferences of bishops in October 1985. The earlier text was removed as part of the modifications requested by the Congregation for Divine Worship when in 1987 it confirmed the decisions of nine English-speaking conferences of bishops to approve the *Order of Christian Funerals.*

24. These two lines are somewhat different from those which appeared in the 1985 text that was presented to the conferences of bishops. The rewording was done after the Congregation for Divine Worship sent its 1987 list of modifications to the conferences.

25. The poem concludes: "God, lover of souls, swaying considerate scales,/ Complete thy creature dear O where it fails,/Being mighty a master, being a father and fond" (*The Poems of Gerard Manley Hopkins,* 4th ed., W. H. Gardner and N. H. Mackenzie, eds. [London: Oxford University Press, 1967] 67–68).

26. DOL 86, no. 639 (19 April 1967).

27. DOL 212, no. 1762 (26 November 1969).

Donald M. Clark

Black Priest. Black Parish. "White" Rite?

Startling events in the spring–summer of 1989 had great impact on the Catholic Church in the United States, and on attentive men and women within the Catholic Church. A priest of the Archdiocese of Washington made yet another public charge of racism within the Church. There was nothing new in that. There would have been nothing particularly arresting in the charge, had that priest not insisted that to redress this long-standing grievance, the Church should create a separate Catholic rite for black people, and he himself intended to establish an African American Catholic congregation.

During those days few, if any, black Catholics stood up to say that racism does not exist in the Catholic Church in the United States, or that the spiritual needs of black people cannot be better met by new forms or worship more consistent with their culture and modes of expression. Black Catholics, in the main, agreed that we have suffered and endured for centuries in a Church that gives unrelenting and clear signs that it does not take us seriously and could be very happy indeed if we just went away! Almost none of us whose skin is dark and whose culture is called "minority culture" in the United States cannot tell "horror stories" of direct contact with overt and covert racist actions by Catholic persons, congregations, religious ministers, Church leaders, policies, laws, practices.

Whether or not a separate rite for African American or black Catholics is the only useful and effective resolution of the Church's racist past or our victimization within it must be debated and decided, not by white people, whether hierarchical or no; nor by white priests who serve among black people; nor by white religious sisters who share pastoral ministry and teach black children in schools. We ourselves, black Catholic people, must consider and decide whether and when such a separate rite may best serve us and what it should include: liturgical and symbolic actions only, or juridical and hierarchical autonomy as well.

This essay will not contribute much to such debates and decisions. These must still go on; I do not know what they will conclude. They may demonstrate that all the "roaring" thus far has been of a single lion, sated by a recent kill—some "progress" has been made, after all!—but the lion will be hungry again, and this time on a range where few antelope remain. A greater sound is yet to be heard!

In this essay, I will attempt to answer a series of questions related to the black Catholic experience:

1. What is a black priest and a black parish in the Catholic Church?
2. How different personally and publicly is being black from being white?
3. Can a black spirituality be conclusively identified, and its foundations, supports, and ingredients clearly articulated?
4. How "white" are the traditions of Catholic worship?
5. What room is there for diversity of expression within the Roman Rite?
6. Is there already a quasi- or pseudo- black or African American Rite in the Catholic Church in the United States?
7. What can white Catholics learn from a black experience of praying the Roman Rite?

WHAT IS A BLACK PRIEST AND A BLACK PARISH?

A large number of Catholics, both white and black, lay public claim to a universality of view that says: "We are all human beings!" "I do not see color, race, difference!" "We are Catholics together; I do not think of you/myself as black!"

Well, I say: "I do not know how it is possible to see me and not to see that I am a black man." To see my six feet, four inch height, my forty pounds of excess weight; my graying, thinning hair; my brown, not blue, eyes; my dimples when I smile—to see all that makes me the man whom people recognize from a distance, or call by name after years of absence, and not see the solid fact about me: that I am an African American man, a black man.

If, however, it is possible, let me tell you that I want you to see me as black because that is how I see myself. It makes a difference! Here, of course, I am not talking about negative stereotypes of black people. I identify myself as one whose racial and cultural roots are in the continent of Africa. I identify with that dark race of humans, thought fit only to be "hewers of wood and drawers of water" by earlier generations, and so enslaved to fell the forests, clear the land, plant the cotton, breed and bear babies, clean and care for and serve others, and all the time to "love" the ones who, without so much as a "by your leave" pressed this station upon us and held us to it.

I know that I am different—not inferior, but different—from the majority population of this country and of the Catholic Church in this country. I can identify and accept my differentness, but I see it as a benefit, because I see diversity, and not uniformity or sameness, as the basic law of nature. Diversity makes for strength, gives depth and interest, and augments meaning and value.

A black priest is a man who sees himself as a member of a victimized and oppressed race, and knows that it is within this context that he, and the people he serves, must live and minister. A black priest and a black parish, are together on this: they admit their difference, their uniqueness apart from the majority society, and they address themselves to the building up of *their* race, *their* economics, *their* communities, *their* spirituality, *their* Catholicism and Catholic expression.

This dedication, even when it is at its most intense, is not anti-white or anti-anyone else. To be a black priest and black parish is to be in favor of, and not to be against. This is one of the hardest lessons for people to learn. Somehow many let themselves be or feel threatened by commitments to persons or causes of which they are not part, or in which they cannot see their interests being served. Particularity within universality has been, and continues to be, essential to Catholicism. The "particular" includes the overtly African American priest and parish, along with the Irish and Polish, the French and German, the Slovak and Hispanic, and all the other national, ethnic, and language groups that are part of "being the Catholic Church."

HOW DIFFERENT PERSONALLY AND PUBLICLY IS BEING BLACK FROM BEING WHITE?

This is not an easy question to answer; and it may well be that whatever answer I give, others will energetically oppose it. Nevertheless, I say there is a difference of worldview between blacks and whites. Different histories, life experiences, cultural bases, and appreciations of future possibilities are involved. Different music, different foods, different sounds, different smells, odors, textures, and emotions distinguish European American and African Americans, and, I may add, Asian and Pacific Americans, from Hispanic and Native Americans.

On a slightly popular TV program this spring, *Equal Justice*, there is a character, an assistant district attorney, who is African American. Obviously intellectually gifted and well-educated in the law, the man is committed and dedicated, passionate and sensitive.

He also loves Italian opera (Verdi and Puccini) and Italian food which he cooks up with skill and authenticity. In fact, the African American actor who plays the part has revealed that in the original script the character he plays was Italian. He applied for the role and was so persuasive that he got it. The name was changed, along with some of the story lines, but some details were left alone.

When the character appears on screen, he is not a black man playing an Italian lawyer, he is an African American lawyer who loves Italian opera and Italian food, but is no less black for that. His blackness comes out "between the lines," in the cracks and crevices of the acting, in the jots and tittles of the scripts: the way he walks, the set of his jaw, the flare of his nostrils, the things that make him laugh, what makes him mad.

One asks the question: why does this black man cook *carbonara* and *osso buco* instead of blackeyed peas and ham hocks? One doesn't ask: why is he so "white"? or, what happened to his African American-ness?

Individuals and groups of persons who are black may be so deeply immersed in various forms of European American culture that the description "cosmopolitan" is aptly applied to them, yet, they retain aspects of the black heritage which comes to expression at various moments and in various ways.

I know people, in fact whole congregations of people, who uncover or discover their black uniqueness in moments of prayer, praise, and worship. They find parts of their souls touched and activated by the music, the songs, the rhythms and cadences of what is often described as "The Black Church." Yet they know the classics of art and music. They wear the clothing of Armani and Brooks Brothers. They thrill to the singing of Price, Estes, Norman, Battle. And they dine on French cuisine with appreciation.

The link between worship and culture is so strong and enduring that even generations, it would seem, do not break it. Neither worship nor culture exist in suspension, in vacuum chambers. Worship is the action of people. And people are cultural beings, who live, move, and exist only in the concrete world of culture which Anscar Chupungo describes as: "the sum total of human values, of social and religious traditions and rituals and of the modes of expression through language and the arts, all of which are rooted in the particular genius of the people" (Chupungo, *Cultural Adaptation of the Liturgy,* 75).

CAN A BLACK SPIRITUALITY BE CONCLUSIVELY IDENTIFIED AND ITS FOUNDATIONS, SUPPORTS, AND INGREDIENTS CLEARLY ARTICULATED?

Whether or not one can identify and articulate the foundations, supports, and ingredients of a black spirituality is something scholars are investigating. Spirituality is so bound to culture and community that, as long as one does not try to impose a rigid uniformity on a whole race of people, so that every black person must conform to a single pattern of thoughts, attitudes, action, etc., I believe certain spiritual qualities and practices applying to African Americans in general can be identified.

It is a spirituality rooted in the Bible, the Hebrew Scriptures in which the creative and liberative God is revealed and the heroic and dependable deeds of salvation proclaimed; the apostolic witness in which God's love, expressed in the incarnate Word Jesus' life, death, and resurrection, is set forth; and finally, the community of beloved, spirit-filled disciples, who preach and pray, heal and deliver, endure suffering and triumph over it in faith. It is a spirituality that is so intensely personal that it shakes one to the depths of one's being and makes one in the core of one's being responsible to God; and it is also communal in that each individual who encounters God in Christ is grafted into a holy people of God, an Israel that is made new. It is a spirituality that is incarnated in the very flesh and blood and soul of black folks, so that the totality of humanness is included: the soaring human spirit, the yearning human heart, the resounding human voice, the deep human silence, the swaying body, the throbbing feet, the clapping hands (and insistent sensuality and sexuality, too); nothing, save sin, is left out or untouched when God's Spirit comes into human spirits and draws from them spiritual expression.

Look into a black church, tune in to the evangelical channel on television, listen to worship in progress while driving past a storefront church, visit a Catholic parish in the urban North. There black spirituality in all its vitality may be given expression, at least in some of its broader outlines.

HOW "WHITE" ARE THE TRADITIONS OF CATHOLIC WORSHIP? There is an assumption in the popular mind that Catholic worship in the Roman Rite is "white" worship. What does that mean? It must mean that it is drawn predominantly from European sources and practices, aimed at the people and cultures of the "white" world, accessible and uplifting to one group but not to others.

It cannot be disputed that the spreading of the Christian Church to the peoples of Europe has profoundly affected Catholic worship. The extant historical studies that document the adaptations of liturgy from the earliest centuries concentrate on the influences brought about by Christian converts of Europe. However, the basic norms of liturgy are Semitic. The word service and the service of sacrifice are Jewish, not European. The litany-style prayers that endure today in the restored Catholic liturgy may owe as much to the desert fathers as to the liturgists of Rome, Gaul, and Germany.

In the end I am loathe to concede too much of the traditions of the Roman Rite to "white" people, at least as we presently designate them. I think a scholarly case can be made for varied, non-white influences upon liturgical practice in the ancient Church, and I think that, while the historical roots may be lost, it is arguable that the ingredients of the Roman Rite are, in fact, universal, that is, truly catholic.

Today, this is my presumption. Even if it shall someday be demonstrated not to be the case, I do not think that African American Christians, including Catholics, are unwilling to accept and build upon rituals of praise and prayer common to the churches. The traditional black Christian churches with which I am familiar follow outlines of Sunday worship that are similar, if not identical, to the ones used in "white" Christian churches. The order of service is the frame that is received and used without apparent concern for the national, ethnic, or racial origins of those who originated it, or who likewise use it.

The "variables" at Christian worship which "customize" it to the congregation need not be the ritual remade wholly. Churches appropriate what may be called the "generic" rites by the types of music and song they choose, the vocal cadences of those who read the Bible in the assembly, the quality, style, and content of the

Sunday preaching, the manifestation of "Spirit gifts" of utterance, swooning, affirmation shouting, public praise, ritual movement or dance, etc.

These things which can be dismissed easily as "incidentals" of worship are, in fact, the very things that distinguish Sunday services according to congregations. If the Church can, with generosity, offer basic structures for worship, and from its centuries-old storehouse present some workable details, while leaving room for cultural adaptations, why insist on more?

IS THERE ALREADY A QUASI- OR PSEUDO- BLACK OR AFRICAN AMERICAN RITE IN THE CATHOLIC CHURCH IN THE UNITED STATES?

This level of openness to adaptation already exists within the Roman Rite for African American Catholics, and for many others as well. Taking the Mass of the Roman Rite as it was reformed according to the principles established by *Sacrosanctum Concilium,* Vatican Council II restored to the Rite "the Roman genius of simplicity of structure and clarity of expression in order to promote active and intelligent participation," as Ansgar Chupungo puts it.

The Bishops' Committee on the Liturgy, NCCB, has gratefully received liturgical variations that grow out of African American traditions in worship; already these are being incorporated into the Roman Rite. *In Spirit and Truth: Black Catholic Reflections on the Order of Mass* was approved and published in 1987–88 for use in the African American Catholic parishes of the country. It is the work of the Black Liturgy subcommittee of the BCL and presents adaptations that are at once "authentically Black and authentically Catholic." In the hands of well-disposed, insightful, and creative black parishes, *In Spirit and Truth* can be the basis for first attempts to adapt the Roman Rite for African American Catholics, similar to the so-called "Zairian Rite" used in Zaire in central Africa. That adaptation is properly called: "the Roman Rite adapted for the people of Zaire." It is, in fact, the same basic ritual used throughout the Latin Catholic Church but with some cultural variations and changes. *In Spirit and Truth* can be similar, *mutatis mutandis,* in our situation here.

Of course, there are some who favor greater and more radical changes in any rituals of worship for African American Catholics. Special preparatory rites that begin before Mass and imitate the deacon-led prayer meeting common in some black Christian churches (cf. *In Spirit and Truth,* 9) are not enough. An entrance procession of ministers (including choir) which is a joy-filled "marching to Zion, the beautiful city of God" is not enough. A carefully balanced repentance rite in the presence of the God who has redeemed us in the blood of Jesus Christ is not enough. The angels' hymn of glory (in the seasons where it is appropriate) concluded with a period of silent prayer is not enough. A "collected" prayer spoken aloud in the name of all present and worshipping is not enough. Even though in an assembly of black Catholics with a black priest presiding all these ritual actions can feel, sound, and be black, they are not enough for some.

There is an articulated need for more radical changes in the preparatory and introductory rites. The calling upon our saintly ancestors, the pouring of libations of wine upon the earth, the introducing of guests and visitors, greetings shared with one another, etc.—an abundance of ritual acts that will prolong the gathering of the assembly and retard its entry into rapt prayer in the presence of the living God is suggested, urged, insisted on.

For some it is not enough that Christ's Church be instructed by the Bible, sacred Scripture, the "two-edged sword" sharp enough to cleave bone and marrow, and dependable because it is the "word coming from the mouth of God." The true African American Catholic Rite needs to hear black authors and poets who are to be read on a par with Scripture.

In a number of parishes since Vatican Council II, assemblies have, often under the leadership of pastors and pastoral ministers, already changed the rites of the Mass. The bishops at the council proscribed such actions. Still, they are done "because no one but the assembly itself has the right to determine how it will worship" (as a pastor in Detroit told me). Or, "because we must resist the rampant sexism in the Church which forbids women's ordination and fuller participation in worship." Or, "because Catholic worship is too 'white,' too European, and the only way we can make it acceptable to black people is by imitating, appropriating what is done in more traditionally black churches" (and this from a priest who has never been to such a church nor studied its forms and their meanings!).

The fact that the Catholic Church, through its bishops, envisioned and required a more orderly adaptation, a studied and tested and evaluated adaptation entered into with prior approval and accepted or rejected after experimentation, and suited to an entire community of communities (not just one or two parishes), has not fazed those who are determined to remake the Catholic Church in an image and likeness more to their own tastes.

Since the practice of worship shapes the beliefs of the worshipers, such practices are already creating new ways of believing. When I ask the question, "Is there already a quasi- or pseudo- Rite for African American Catholics in the United States?" it is in light of these facts that I ask. Reviewing what I and others know to be happening in several dioceses, I conclude that there is! I do not think it is alarmist to say so. The rituals thus created are being celebrated by a number of generations who will be shaped in accordance with their prayer and practice. And the authority to act in these ways—which is usurped authority—is already setting up supposed juridical powers parallel to those of bishops, liturgical scholars and commissions, and even the community of black Catholics.

WHAT CAN WHITE CATHOLICS LEARN FROM THE BLACK EXPERIENCE OF PRAYING THE ROMAN RITE?

Learning is not the point!

White Catholics may discover that the Roman Rite gives us the genius of simplicity and order which can be embellished, modified, and adapted by us to our cultures and traditions. They can discover that the Rite itself does not hinder its energetic use by black (or any other) people. What hinders is slavish, unimaginative, careless, ugly, and spiritless performance of the Rite.

If one has ever been part of a community at prayer, a community that is authentically Catholic and black, one can experience with feeling the presence of God, the redemption in Jesus Christ, the power of the Holy Spirit.

Experience with feeling! Though liturgy is instructive, that is, an activity that teaches, it is not didactic in the sense of being a set pattern for imparting information or stimulating ideas. The Roman Rite celebrated by African American Catholics is **worship**. All who are part of it have an experience; and, insofar as experience often teaches, worshippers may "learn."

I maintain that they experience God. They experience community and communal praising, personal sanctification. They experience themselves being pierced to the heart and laid open to individual challenge and conversion. What white Catholics "learn" in black celebrations of the Roman Rite will be the searing feelings that are part of the experience.

I know how such feeling works upon the worshipper. I have been at St. Henry Church in Cleveland when the assembly at prayer and Fr. J.-Glenn Murray entered into an ecstatic moment when time and place fell away and God was all that mattered. This happened at a Eucharist on the Second Sunday in Ordinary Time (14 January 1990). It happened at Mass, following strictly the Roman Rite with adaptations suggested by *In Spirit and Truth.* Anyone present and fully, consciously, and actively participating was swept along in the assembly. White Catholics or black, old or young, rejoicing or mourning—we all experienced the feeling, and we all learned something.

I can name other churches where similar encounters take place each week in African American Catholic assemblies within the Roman Rite, following—sometimes more, sometimes less—the adaptations suggested in *In Spirit and Truth.* I know other Catholic churches, too, churches that attempt radical reforms of the Rite in an effort to be more "authentically black." I have not found these attempts persuasive, though they may be engaging to many who worship together often. They are idiosyncratic, often crammed with political or ideological cant, theologically and liturgically questionable, and even inconsistent with the ecclesial practices that exist in those black Protestant churches which they attempt to imitate and from which the rituals are supposed to be drawn.

For example: pastors in black churches that I know do not abdicate their responsibilities as leaders of worship and preachers of the Word of God to private persons in the congregation. Black churches do not engage in such spontaneity at worship that the order of service changes markedly from week to week, or that any individual within the assembly is free to do anything that comes to him or her (despite the claim to be so led by the Holy Spirit). Further, recognizing that political matters are part of the "stuff of life," and that those who are living cannot be ignorant of nor unconcerned about such matters, the black church has managed to keep clearly in mind a higher wisdom and a better morality, and not to become lost in the quagmire of political argument and debate on "God's time."

I close with a parable.

Donald M. Clark

There was a girl whose mother was an excellent cook. The mother had a collection of iron skillets, battered stainless pots, aluminum pans, enamelware roasters, copper kettles, and chipped ceramic bowls. These were scarred and pitted from years of use; but, when Mother "got busy" with them, the kitchen smelled like "home" and she always turned out food that was "good for the soul."

When the girl became a woman and married, she received elegant cookware: *Cuisinart, Calphalon,* matched tempered glass bowls, and so forth. Everything was new, bright, and shining.

When she and her husband invited their parents to the first "sit down dinner" in their new home after the wedding, they both feared that their culinary efforts would not measure up to those of their parents. When the company came and the table was set and the matched and coordinated dishes uncovered, behold, the smell of home and food that was "good for the soul," food such as mothers make.

What, do you suppose, is a fitting lesson in this tale?

Elaine Ramshaw

Ritual and Pastoral Care: The Vital Connection

Despite what so many of our carefully organized ministry programs—with well-defined and clearly differentiated responsibilities—may seem to suggest, ritual and pastoral care are not separate activities which must be brought into a carefully negotiated relation, like spending time with your children and making a living. Rather, they each involve the other necessarily, so that one without the other is no more than a caricature of itself. Liturgy without pastoral care is bad liturgy, and pastoral care dissociated from ritual and symbol is perhaps good psychotherapy, but certainly deficient pastoral care.

Unfortunately, these caricatures exist all around us. We all know people who perform some aspects of pastoral care well, are good at counseling or facilitating group process, but have no sense of ritual. Perhaps they are uncomfortable with ritual leadership, or tonedeaf to the music of symbols. Congregations often are loyal to such ministers out of gratitude for their personal caring, and spend an hour on Sunday morning wincing or dozing or planning a laypeople's takeover of the liturgical planning process. If they put up with such a minister's liturgical clinkers, it may be because they have experienced the opposite caricature: the person who is invested in liturgical performance but who lacks the most basic pastoral sensitivity. These are the people who preside with rubrical correctness over generic, fill-in-the-blank funerals, where the deceased is buried in impersonal prayers before being interred.

Even more common are those who try to practice both good liturgy and sensitive pastoral care, but who end up subordinating one concern to the other. On the one side are those who force their pastoral care into a ritual straitjacket: for example, well-meaning pastors who use prayer in hospital visits to paper over with all-purpose pious phrases the questions raised by suffering. (In fact, they often unconsciously use prayer simply as a way to get out the door!) On the other side are ministers who subordinate ritual to their understanding of pastoral care, seeing ritual as a "pastoral hook" which must be used according to therapeutic norms: for example, the CPE supervisor, telling seminarians to baptize a dead baby if the parents request it, because "it doesn't make any difference to the baby, and it will make the parents feel better." It is possible to argue for baptizing stillborn infants with a care for sacramental integrity; but this particular rationale clearly indicates the triumph of the therapeutic. An even clearer example is the account (published in *Christian Century* not long ago) of a "memorial service for Isaac," in which "Isaac" was the name assigned to the wished-for but wholly nonexistent child of an infertile couple.

These examples point to a confusion between the private world of fantasy, to which therapy grants reality on its own terms, and the public world of shared reality and meaning-making, where Christian ritual belongs. One could have such a "memorial service" within the therapy hour, with the individuals and their therapist symbolizing the inner world; but any public ritual would have to distinguish a dream from a fetus and certainly from a baby. A more cohesive approach, combining the norms and concerns of liturgy and pastoral care, may lead to a rite of passage focused explicitly on the couple, in which they mourn their identity as prospective parents and turn to a new self-definition as a couple, to other possible vocations, other avenues of generativity.

How do pastoral ministers move towards such a cohesive approach to human need? How do we make the necessary connection between ritual and pastoral care? This vital task has two sides. First, we must attend to the human experience of the need, the capacity for ritual and the effects of ritual. Second, we must live our way more deeply into the Christian symbols, the language of liturgy, so that we can bring those symbols to human experience without reducing or distorting experience.

We attend to the human experience of the need and capacity for ritual in both formal and informal ways. Informally, pastors and other Christian ministers are always intuiting persons' needs with untrained, "natural" empathy, or hearing them with the trained ear of a counselor. Some aspects of human ritual experience, however, will only reveal themselves to a formal analysis, such as the studies of individual or systemic phenomena carried out by the social sciences. I propose to look first at three areas in which psychology makes contributions to the understanding of ritual need and practice, and then turn to contributions from sociology and social theory.

THE HUMAN EXPERIENCE: THE CONTRIBUTIONS OF PSYCHOLOGY

1. Psychology sheds light, first of all, on human development. The cognitive psychologists, such as Piaget, help us see how people construct the meaning of rituals for themselves at different ages, how they work with abstract or concrete symbols, how they perceive the explanations proffered them. Erikson's psychosocial theory (and other theories of the life cycle) lift up the concerns, abilities, and needs of people in the various stages of life, providing a shifting context for ritual in the individual's life. Small children need an orderly and trustworthy world, according to Erikson, a need which is met by dependable interaction with adult ritualizers. Older children are ready for intentional participation in the wider community, for things they can learn to do competently. The need of adolescents to forge an identity independent of parents is expressed in part through impressive spontaneous ritual-making; careful study of such rituals can inform the Church's attempts to provide ritual markers for adolescent growth in faith. Adults form and break up intimate relationships, often without formal social rituals, and face the shock of becoming a ritualizer for the next generation. The elderly have both the need and (in health) the capacity to tell their stories in a way that will be received beneficially by the young. The findings of psychology continue to point up the changing needs and capacities of the human life cycle. Relying upon such analysis, we can identify the transitions in life that need to be midwifed by ritual, and thus develop a ritual practice which actively engages people throughout the life cycle with their own developmental issues as well as the developmental issues of others with whom they are in relationship.

2. The second area illumined by psychological analysis is that of unconscious mental processes. Ritual functions on both the conscious and unconscious levels of meaning. Unconscious mental processes are meaningful, though they have a logic quite alien to the conscious mind. Therefore, when ritual "works" on an unconscious level, it works by meaning, by signifying something to our unconscious mind, and not merely, for instance, by providing a cathartic acting out of an affect detached from meaning. Thus the meaning of rituals and their symbols for the unconscious mind requires careful investigation.

One place to begin this investigation is with the formation of the God-image in early childhood. Ana-Maria Rizzuto and John McDargh have studied the process by which a child forms an internal representation of God from her experience of the significant adults in her life. Though they allow that the God-representation can be modified by the experiences of later life, they believe that the God-image formed in early childhood is foundational and has a great deal of staying-power. Any liturgist would be chastened by an awareness of the complexity of the individual God-images in the minds of the congregation. For how many in the congregation is the explicit picture of God conveyed in the ritual canceled out by the more powerful God-image from their personal past? A greater respect for the influence of early childhood experience on one's image of God, and a broader understanding of how that God-image persists and develops throughout life, largely on an unconscious level, is an essential first step.

The actions and concrete symbols of a ritual will also have unconscious levels of meaning. The primal nature of our central sacramental actions ensures that they will resonate on unconscious as well as conscious levels. The deep patterns of our experience of eating and being fed and feeding others will play into our experience of the Eucharist. Psychoanalytic studies show us that these deep patterns are not simple or universal (though they have common elements), but highly individualized and complex. In Marguerite Sechehaye's classic account of her treatment of a schizophrenic girl, the "symbolic realizations" of the title, *Ritual Enactments in Therapy,* include two kinds of feeding. Sechehaye feeds the anorexic girl apple slices by hand, which she experiences as breast-feeding; and she also feeds her whipped cream, a purifying "snow" which silences the self-punitive voices within her. The power of these feeding rituals to affect the girl's conscious and unconscious world is vividly portrayed. Such unconscious meanings may be closer to the surface in a schizophrenic person, but they are present in all human beings.

An unpublished essay on the unconscious meaning of the sacraments by the French psychotherapist Sr. Marie Bernard Chicaud ("Fantasy and the Sacraments of Penance and the Eucharist") tells the stories of two children (not emotionally disturbed): a boy who got depressed and stopped eating before his first confession, and a girl who got sick on her first communion day. She discusses various fantasies and fears that can be aroused by the sacraments.

After exploring these unconscious meanings, she suggests a number of guidelines for catechists. "Above all," she says, "it is necessary to listen carefully to the child in this matter and to lead him to express himself on the meaning and the consequences for him when he is to participate in the Body of Christ." If there are anxieties, they must be taken seriously. Clarifications may help, or the teacher may be able to help the child to find a way to deal with his fears in conversation or in play. Things may work out if the child is allowed to approach the sacrament in his own time. Chicaud argues for an individualized approach to the timing of first Communion. Finally, Chicaud raises the issue of the teacher's self-awareness. She thinks that catechists and pastors should be aware of their own fantasies about the sacraments—a subject not included in the curriculum of most seminaries. While this essay focuses on the fearful fantasies that cause problems for children, one has to remember that the unconscious meanings of liturgical symbols are positive as well as negative, and either way contribute to the power of the sacrament in our lives.

Do unconscious meanings (operative or not) raise issues in the pastoral liturgical care of psychologically healthy adults? Consider the controversy in many churches over the use of the common cup. Many American adults resist the common cup because, they say, of the risk of contagion. Curiously, however, a number of congregations have compromised, using a chalice with a pouring lip. Those who wish drink directly from the chalice; others take the wine poured into individual cups. How did the latter accept this compromise, when it seems to defeat the purpose of hygiene? My contention is that this betrays the basis of the original objection in less rational, unconscious fears of physical intimacy and contamination, fears for which the contagion theory provided a rationale. In other words, it is not the fear of germs but the refusal to put my lips where others have put theirs. Hence the practical, pastoral significance of recognizing the role of unconscious meanings: no amount of scientific evidence on the risk of contagion will do any good, and seemingly irrational approaches may succeed where reason is doomed to fail.

One important arena in which we continually confront the unconscious is that of gender. In the congregation I belong to we are currently discussing whether to use the *Lectionary for the Christian People,* which not only removes sexist references to humanity but also avoids calling God "he." The force of the emotional reaction from some who are opposed to this—none of whom is a biblical fundamentalist, and all of whom would intellectually agree that God transcends gender—has been quite impressive. They seem to regard this as a direct attack upon their God-representation, and thus upon their faith. Similar strong unconscious forces are encountered in the debate over women's ordination. Many things are felt without being said or even consciously formulated. A man may feel that accepting the authority of a woman returns him to childhood, or that the pastor's being a woman means that religion really is "womanish." A woman may have her own ambivalence about women in authority, due to rivalry with her mother or to the relinquishment of her own wishes for power and recognition. Or she may vote against calling a woman pastor because the pastor has been the only man in her life who touches her and cares about her. We need to be more honest about the sexual dynamics in ritual, as well as in the rest of Church life.

A final issue regarding the role of the unconscious is a concern which lies between psychology and medicine: the function of the placebo effect in healing. The placebo effect is a change in one's health caused by something which is not an "active agent" in biomedical terms. If your faith in your doctor heals you, that's a placebo effect; the same can be said for your faith in God. As we learn more about the relationship between mind and body, in the field of psychoneuroimmunology and such practices as the use of imagery in healing, the placebo effect is less easily dismissed. Future discussions of the meaning of our rituals and prayers for the sick should not go on without dialogue with these new findings. Such dialogue would not have to lead to either magical or secularized understandings of a rite of healing; rather, it could help attune us to God's ways of healing us, not only through body chemistry, but also through the workings of the unconscious mind.

3. In addition to human development and the unconscious, psychology also helps us understand the dynamics of family systems. Family systems theory provides an important perspective from which to view ritual, along with the rest of the Church's life. In the last decade, family systems theorists have turned their attention to family rituals. They study a family's customary rituals (e.g., how they celebrate holidays) for diagnostic purposes. They also experiment with ritual as a means of intervention in family therapy,

modifying existing rituals or creating new ones in an attempt to change the family's patterns of interaction. A psychologist at Children's Hospital in Columbus described a ritual intervention. The "identified patient" was a six-year-old boy, about whom his family could see nothing good. When he was in the womb, his mother's brother, a feared and despised man, had died; and the family was afraid that the uncle's spirit had possessed the little boy. The therapists had the family write down on slips of paper all the qualities they had seen in the uncle, and now feared finding in the boy. These slips of paper were ceremonially burned and the ashes buried. Then the therapists had the family construct a new, positive image of the boy, with qualities they would like to see. The psychologist explained with considerable awe the effects of this ritual on the family. It was like night and day, he said. Before, they picked up only on the bad things; after, they saw a wonderful child. The mother could not say enough good about him. This is not to suggest that pastoral ministers should begin interfering with family rituals without training and supervision. But the example does raise possibilities of what one might do, for example, when an unchurched couple comes to ask for the baptism of their baby because they think he is possessed by the devil.

These situations are helpful in revealing that the work of family therapists in the area of ritual illuminates the effects of ritual on the whole system, not just on the individuals within the system.

Systems Theory. Systems theory is a good bridge between psychology and the other social sciences that provide formal analyses of human ritual: sociology, cultural anthropology, and social theory. Liturgiologists have studied anthropology more thoroughly than psychology. They have made extensive use of the helpful paradigm from the work of Arnold van Gennep and Victor Turner on the phases of rites of passage. Laurence Hoffman makes use of Mary Douglas's categories of analysis of groups and their ways of symbolizing. Undoubtedley, anthropologists like Margaret Mead and Clifford Geertz through their research have influenced liturgical studies.

Less attention, however, has been paid to popular culture studies, the sociological studies of our own culture. What is the ritual life of contemporary Americans? How do people ritualize in our culture? Popular culture studies analyze the rituals of public life (sports, politics, the entertainment media) as well as those of private life (family holidays, life transitions). No Christian marriage manual will tell how people really ritualize the process of marrying in America; only studies of popular culture will tell that. Jessica Mitford's *The American Way of Death* probably did more to initiate critical thinking about funeral practices than did the liturgical movement.

Where are new rituals being created, and what does that tell us about the need for ritual? Bereaved parents' support groups are developing rituals for miscarriage, twelve-step groups are ritualizing their spiritual discipline, noncustodial parents re-ritualize holidays, and feminist couples work at nonsexist pre-wedding parties. Where do people try but seemingly fail to ritualize? Questions such as these are important for the Church as it frames its pastoral liturgical practice. An effective liturgical practice will resonate with the ritual practice of the culture. The Church cannot provide for every human ritual need (nor would this be desirable), but there are times when it can add a blessing to a secular ritual, or influence the shape and content of Christian ritualizing outside church walls. This may mean providing rituals where there are none, or at least providing the resources for those who are developing rituals to address their own situations. In any case, the Church should be aware that its liturgies are not celebrated in a ritual void. We cannot think intelligently about weddings, for instance, until we recognize that the Church service is only one element in a complex ritual process, carrying messages that may be quite contrary to the Church's values regarding economics, gender roles, and the nature of family.

Critical Social Theory and Feminism. In a similar vein, we have much to learn from both critical social theory and feminism. We need to take seriously the social, economic, and gender infrastructure of our liturgical symbol system. How is the economic power structure reflected in ritual practice? Who leads? Who is listened to? Who decides what happens within a given liturgy? Which vocations are ritually honored and which are not? Does the community cross class lines? How is money spent for the ritual, and how does it function as a symbol within it? In the Lutheran church of my childhood, on a normal Sunday without communion, the object treated with the most reverence was the collected money: it alone was carried in procession and elevated before the altar. Apart from the singing, the collection was the most participatory activity. How are the economic realities of people's lives referred to and symbolized? How are issues of social justice, including economic inequity, raised in the liturgical context?

A similar set of questions can be raised from the standpoint of feminism. How is gender symbolized in language and action? What activities or roles are performed only by members of one gender (for example, washing the communion ware)? How are patriarchal power structures reflected in ritual forms? When my relative Linda went touring as part of a panel that spoke to Episcopal churches on the ordination of women (before ordination was approved in that denomination) she encountered the whole gamut of objections, from rational arguments from tradition to irrational arguments from menstruation. But almost always, she said, after the more sensible objections had been addressed, some man would ask, "But what if she's attractive? Wouldn't that be distracting?" The temptation, Linda said, was to respond, "Well, what do you think has been happening to *us* all these years?" But that response would only elicit shock and disapproval from the men who asked this question. "What's wrong with you, that you had sexual thoughts in church?" The underlying thought process clearly went like this: If a man were leading the liturgy, and a woman felt attracted to him, that was because the woman brought sex into the situation. ("After all," the man thinks, "*I* never felt there was anything sexual there.") On the other hand, if a woman is leading the liturgy, and a man feels attracted to her, that is because the woman brings sex into the situation. Only a critical theory of gender will illuminate the history and ramifications of the symbol behind this thinking—the identification of woman with sexuality. This is why we need feminism: not only as a philosophical argument for change but also as a critical analysis of the unspoken assumptions of our current liturgical practice.

THE CHRISTIAN SYMBOLS: CONTRIBUTIONS FROM SOCIOLOGY AND SOCIAL THEORY

These formal analyses contribute to one side of the task of connecting ritual and pastoral care: that of attending to the human experience of ritual. This vital task has another side, equally important. We must live our way more deeply into the Christian symbols, so that we can bring those symbols to human experience without reducing or distorting it. Only then will the symbols have the power to transform or illuminate our experience.

First, in order to allow the symbols to speak more deeply, we must overcome a number of factors that have limited their semantic range and prevented them from making contact with large areas of experience. First, we must work to overcome the biases of class, race, and gender. Usually, the best way to do this is not to eliminate symbols, although there may be certain formulations that strike us as too oppressive to use once our consciousness has been raised. More often, though, other approaches are more constructive. We can add other symbols, whether recovered from the tradition, adopted from the culture, or newly devised. We can work at turning symbols on their heads, as Jesus did, with parable, paradox, and humor: the good brother is the obstructionist, the outsider is the neighbor, the master is the servant. And we can take the cross seriously—not as an icon of self-negation, but as the human cost of choosing the outsider, the divine value of what is most vulnerable.

Second, we must overcome dualisms of nature and spirit, body and soul, this-worldly and otherworldly. Our prayers, hymns, and liturgies have astonishingly little of the natural world in them, and what there is is often pastoral and romanticized—all rainbows and butterflies and "wheat that springeth green." We need more real nature in our worship life: nature with its terror as well as its beauty, its fragility as well as its vitality. The liturgical movement's advocacy of large fonts with visible water and real bread made by human hands has helped reconnect our prayer with the natural world; so also has the concern for social justice, which reminds us that God cares about the physical conditions of people's lives. The spiritualizing tendency, nevertheless, is deeply ingrained in Christianity, and must be continually challenged if our symbols are to relate to people as more than disincarnate souls.

From a pastoral care perspective, perhaps the heritage of Stoicism is even more problematic for Western Christianity than the nature/spirit dualism. The Church always officially repudiated dualism, no matter how persistently popular theology fell victim to it. The doctrines of the goodness of creation and the resurrection of the body have acted as a check on rampaging dualism. There has been no such repudiation, however, of the Stoic ethics of human feeling. The Church Fathers assumed that the stoic norms of moderation and rational control were compatible with Christian views. Consequently, the Stoic suspicion of all strong feeling, including rage, sexual passion, and even grief, has been carried on in Christian anthropology. Christian letters of consolation from the sixteenth century are exactly like the letters of Stoic philosophers in form of argument; only the reasons adduced for the arguments are Christianized. Words are placed in the mouth of the deceased, who tells the mourner to moderate his or her grief. As a result of such Stoic tendencies, we have little or no room in our ritual/symbol system for legitimate anger or for sexual feeling, and sadness or fear are often cast as a lack of faith. There can hardly be any greater obstacle to connecting ritual and pastoral care than the fact that our liturgies ignore or stigmatize so much of natural human feeling.

Last spring there was a serious fire at night in one of the dorms on my seminary's campus, and the alarm system didn't function. Luckily, a few people coming home late managed to get everyone out of the building; otherwise the students might have died of smoke inhalation. Later, we held a special worship service focusing on the experience of the fire and its aftermath; I was struck by how the service was dominated by the note of gratitude. Surely there was gratitude, in light of what could have and didn't happen; but there were many other feelings as well. There was a bidding prayer in which people were invited to participate aloud, and after several people offered prayers of gratitude I said, "For all the people, especially the children, who are afraid to go to sleep these nights. Where are you in our nightmares, God?" When the service was over two people separately came to thank me for that prayer. I hadn't done anything except say what was in my heart—and theirs. But that simple act is often impossible in our liturgies.

Recover and Shape Anew. As we struggle against the class, race, and gender biases, the dualism, and the Stoicism that warp and narrow our symbols, we can also work to recover the symbolic richness available to us in the tradition and to shape new ritual symbols out of our time and culture. Recovering the richness of traditional Christian symbols has been one of the main goals of the liturgical movement, with its insistence on the use of full sacramental symbols and its reclaiming of ritual process. In a similar vein Gail Ramshaw contends that we need to reappropriate the ancient use of story and symbol as typology—not in the anti-Judaic mode where all is an inferior shadow of Christ, but in the sense of the layering of images like so many transparencies over a map or a chart of the human body. The *Easter Sourcebook,* coedited by Gail Ramshaw and Gordon Lathrop, is a wonderful primer in this typological language of the liturgy, with each week of the Easter season assigned a cluster of images for salvation. The quotations supporting each image are drawn from centuries of Christian history, and demonstrate the flexible and often surprising ways the symbols have been used. But in addition to recovering symbolic riches from the past, we may need to adapt symbols or shape new ones for our time and culture. I get a sense of awe from reading good science writing that I never get from the liturgy. Can we make connections between that scientific wonder and our worship life? The cosmos actually seems much smaller to me in church, limited to the human scale. Many have experienced radical grace in therapy; yet therapy has never been held up in any liturgy I have attended as an icon of redemption. What would it mean to the adult survivor of incest if the Church talked about God as resembling not only a father but also a therapist? It might help her to see God, not in her enslavement, but in her exodus and homecoming.

Praying the Symbols. Finally, of course, we live our way more deeply into the Christian symbols by praying them, and by helping each other to find ways to pray them. In a workshop for parents on family ritual, I begin by asking them how they ritualize their family lives now, how time is structured and how special times are marked. Then we talk about the religious ritual they perform, if any, and about the religious ritual performed in their families of origin. What feels good, what feels bad, and why? If the class stretches over several weeks, I get them to ask their parents the same questions about their families of origin, and why they made the decisions they did about what to do in the families they established. I talk with them about many different styles of family ritual, from reading Bible stories to sharing a blessing cup to singing at bedtime to drawing pictures together.

We discuss which sort of prayer may be most successfully grafted onto each family's unique ritual life. In all of this I try to do two things: to attend to the human experience of ritual in these families, and to enlarge their symbolic repertoire, both by suggesting alternatives and, even more, by encouraging their creativity.

CONCLUSION

When we listen carefully to human experience and when we present symbols that are adequate to that experience, there is potential for pastoral liturgical care that is truly transformative of people's lives. I would like to end with one of my favorite ritual-and-pastoral-care stories. It concerns a seven-year-old girl living with her brother and mother after her parents' divorce. She was seeing things at night in her house. Things got so bad that she would only sleep in her room if the door was wide open, and if she could get completely under the covers. Eventually her mother provided one of those tents that fits on top of a bed, and she would get out from under the covers if she was inside the tent. But the fear of the ghosts or whatever she saw got worse and worse. Her pastor decided to plan a house blessing with the family, and the four of them did the ritual together. They walked from room to room throughout the house, with the brother carrying the Bible, the mother carrying a bowl of water for baptism, and the girl carrying a candle. In each room they talked about what went on in that room, read a Bible passage, sprinkled water, and said a prayer. On my advice, they made sure to include the bathrooms, which are excluded from the Lutheran house blessing ritual. In fact, they ceremonially flushed the toilets. They anointed the front and back doors, and wrote over them the traditional Eastern inscription of the three kings. When they had finished at the back door, the pastor said to the girl, "They're gone now; they simply aren't allowed in here any more." The girl said, "That's that!" and blew out her candle. And that *was* that. They took down the tent, and she slept with the door closed from then on. I know this sounds like magic, but I like to think of it, in the words of C. S. Lewis's *The Lion, the Witch, and the Wardrobe*, as the Deeper Magic from before the Dawn of Time. I'm all for it. What really happened here? In part, the community took a child's experience seriously, and responded to it as a community—the whole family with the pastor as representative of the church. The child was given an active role to play in the symbolic defeat of her fears. And the connection was made between the authentic experience of need and symbols large enough to contain and address that need. The vital connection was made, I feel sure, between ritual and pastoral care.

Paul J. Philibert, O.P.

Human Development and Sacramental Transformation

On Saturday evening, shortly before 8:30, I stood in the square before the Church of San Egidio meeting members of the community gathered for their Pentecost Eucharist, waiting for the liturgy to begin. San Egidio is a lay community in Trastevere, a poor section of Rome, which was founded in 1968 to implement the vision of Vatican II; its special emphasis is lay ministry and care for the poor. Shortly after 8:30 the doors of the church opened and the several hundred parishioners who had gathered in the square filed into a beautifully decorated, dimly illumined church where the choir was singing and candles burned before the many icons in various places. I was greeted, offered a headset for simultaneous translation of the sermon, shown the songbooks, and led to a comfortable seat. The community entered an environment already potent with spiritual energy and already attuned to the celebration of the mystery of the Holy Spirit.

Even with the exquisite chanting and hymns of largely Byzantine inspiration, the highpoint of this liturgy was the inspired preaching of one of the lay founders and leaders of the San Egidio community. The universal prayer, which lasted almost twenty minutes, included petitions offered in German, Spanish, French, and English as well as Italian. A group of five priests concelebrated the sung Eucharistic Prayer which included frequent song responses by the congregation. An *agape* supper followed in the church garden, where people gathered in distinct language groups in leisurely conversation and attentive hospitality.

From beginning to end the community of San Egidio treated me—and everyone else—as an esteemed member of the body of Christ and as a privileged, welcome guest. By contrast, an experience at a parish in downtown Patterson, N.J., stands out in my memory. I had been asked to preach a mission appeal. The pastor, eager to get away, abandoned the rectory as soon as I appeared. No one had informed me that the congregation of the 9:00 A.M. Mass was Spanish-speaking; it was only half-way through the homily that it dawned on me that I was not connected to them linguistically. Many of the congregation prayed the rosary throughout; many others looked glazed over. As soon as I gave the blessing at the end of Mass, the congregation dashed out, well before I reached the back door of the church in an effort to greet the people. A small, elderly Puerto Rican woman brought me an ivory elephant on a silver chain and asked me to bless it as I stood near the door. And I thought: this makes as much sense as anything else I've been doing for the last hour; why not?

From one point of view, these two communities used the same symbols and the same rites. But at San Egidio's we were celebrating lives being changed, while in Patterson we were celebrating the emptiness of lives desperate for some alternative. These two communities represent for me two extremes: one embracing the ordinary and transforming it, the other anxious to escape the ordinary and discard it. These could also be called two images of ministry: one humanizing pastoral care, the other dehumanizing.

Sacramental life requires believers who have been awakened to the mystery that their own lives are signs of faith. In the following pages, I will demonstrate that the dominant forces of our present culture create obstacles to our awakening to this mystery. Then I will suggest that a certain kind of generative spirit is required on the part of Christian ministers to invite people to move beyond the influences of the media culture and to respond to the deepest dynamics of the Christian life. Christian sacraments are not supernatural commodities, but rather gestures of awareness of lives changed and transformed. Likewise Christian pastoral care is the mutual service of God's people as they awaken to the reality of a world penetrated by God's merciful and healing love. In the last analysis, it is Christian communities of mutual service and joyful sharing of life in its wholeness that manifest the transformation of Christ's resurrection life.

INFLUENCES FROM THE CULTURE

Criticism of our contemporary culture has begun to illuminate some of the weaknesses of our strong technological tendency. Our capacities for communication, comfort, and affluence in North America today would have been unimaginable centuries ago. We are blessed by our technology and affluence. What we have done with these gifts and what they have done to us, however, are issues of some significance as we look at our Christian symbolic life. Many critics (Christopher Lasch, Robert Bellah, Richard Bernstein, and others) feel that the payoff of our achievements is not altogether positive,[1] but that they have a shadow side.

Our social order is marked by three powerfully determining influences, especially in America. These are individualism, capitalism, and privatism. In some ways, each of these flaws derives from the same source, namely, the notion of "autonomy" which developed from Enlightenment philosophy. To be reasonable is to be autonomous. To be autonomous is to be independent. To be independent is to be free of concern for others' predicaments. Granted, one will not find that argument in the writings of Immanuel Kant or John Locke or Benjamin Franklin. Rather, these attitudes are the pragmatic results of a popular appropriation of Enlightenment vision.

The obvious move of our ancestors two centuries ago was out from under the sway of royal tyranny. In the eighteenth century, both in England and in France, a caste system of "estates" created a huge underclass that worked slavishly to produce the wealth that allowed the privilege of the rich. Eighteenth century revolutionary theory devised a philosophy of "rights" which assigned to each individual equal status before the law, whatever the individual's wealth or family heritage. In July 1989, Parisians celebrated the two-hundredth anniversary of the French Revolution, that moment when the fate of European monarchs was decided definitively. Enlightenment individualism, as a rebellion against medieval caste, is understandable; it is a noble heritage. But it is also a flawed dream, because it carries within it the seeds of our separateness and competition. In cutting away from the oppressive institutions of eighteenth-century monarchy, the Revolution severed contact with the age-old images of human solidarity rooted in blood and experience. The sort of belonging that links families together, that provides bonds of loyalty to neighborhood and parish, was dissolved in the wash of individualism.[2]

Enlightenment autonomy facilitated competition; competition flowered into capitalism; and we have elaborated capitalism into a form of narcissism. Advanced contemporary capitalism measures the worth of persons in terms of their possessions and their power: money is power in contemporary American society. That power can be used philanthropically (as we have often seen in this century) but the power of money can also be the basis of a perverted anthropology. To the degree that we judge the value of persons according to their money or their social privilege, to the same degree we have a perverted moral vision. An obvious example of the influence of capitalist morality is the preoccupation of our youth with status derived from expensive clothing or even more expensive audio equipment. A conscience formed by capitalist moral education will spontaneously frame social issues competitively. Human worth and dignity become swallowed up in the concerns of individuals' insatiable craving for status.

Traditional religion, in fact, supported the repressive regimes against which Enlightenment thinking reacted. As a consequence, the mass culture today avoids religious issues like poison. A foundational tenet of American constitutional philosophy was the separation of religion and politics. William Buckley is reported to have said that people who mention religion more than once at a cocktail party in America can be sure they will never be invited back again. Religion has become a private issue, just as we have privatized all ultimate issues. It is impolite to ask questions about the fundamental ground of value or belief upon which we build our lives. Such questions may make others uncomfortable.

To summarize then, individualism, narcissism, and privatism as found in North American society today are a corruption of the Enlightenment ideals of the Age of Revolution. Probably the rough and tumble spirit of free enterprise in the confused decades of European immigration to America had as much to do with the shape of America today as its public philosophy. In any case, these are the dominant influences in these later decades of the twentieth century.

Individualism even overpowers religion and values. Though religion must bear the burden of relating the whole cosmos to its Creater-Source, it is perceived as a matter of individual conscience. Religious people today, unfortunately, are more preoccupied with "my heaven" than "God's kingdom." Despite twenty-five years of preaching that social justice is an integral part of evangelization, the Church has scarcely made a dent in the individualistically oriented piety of the majority of its communicants.

The narcissism of the popular culture is perhaps clearest in the contemporary focus on self-conscious experience. Courses in meditation and self-hypnotism for the pursuit of serenity are a growth industry—and not just in California. Within Roman Catholicism, there is a new wave of Marian visionaries whose teachings and visions promise security, usually in exchange for a pilgrimage and a pledge of private devotions. The security and complacency of the self (narcissistic reflection) lie at the bottom of these a-social movements. In the general culture, advertising both fosters and profits from the public's inability to distinguish between whims and needs. The narcissistic forces of society infect Christian consciousness so that the last thing one would expect to find in the average Catholic church is prophetic preaching. The Church has been coopted into behaving like one more franchise in the Human Potential movement.

The privatism of our society places a taboo on public discussion of religious experience. Granted, religious experience is the hardest single thing in the world to talk about; but when the celebration of a parish community is utterly void of concrete reference to the way God's grace is at work in its families and its people's lives, then it becomes a dry, abstract formality. Indeed what we find very often are wordy celebrations that do everything possible to keep the messy reality of broken and healing lives in domesticated control. We fear physical intimacy; we fear feeling; we fear ecstasy. How fascinating that St. Thomas Aquinas thought that feeling is the concrete integration of nature, desire, and the good, and that without feeling and delight, virtue is deficient. We are meant to be motives of celebration for one another,[3] but the privatizing taboo of our society paralyzes us before we can share the faith stories that are our witness to a living God. It is no wonder that so many Americans seek compensation for this lack of feeling in public life by indulging in the artificial passion of TV soap operas.

It is probably too strong to claim that individualism, narcissism, and privatism, effects of latter-day Enlightenment thinking, constitute a kind of ersatz religion, though they almost universally govern the concerns and values of the mass media in America today. Still they are not ultimate values, but rather a refusal to consider ultimate values. What is involved is not so much an alternative religion as an abdication of concern for ultimacy. When respectable people almost universally think that religion is silly, it becomes very difficult for those who are the ministers of religion to make a case for the penetrating power of grace throughout all dimensions of human life.

To raise the question of pastoral care in this culture, then, first of all demands that we recognize that the patterns just described constitute a cultural sickness. The care we need would address the dimensions of this sickness. How might we be able to do this?

CHURCH AS A HEALING PRESENCE

If individualism, narcissism, and privatism are the sickness, then the Church heals by revealing itself as an authentic human community. This revelation takes the veil away from the illusions of the Enlightenment myth. When we can accept the woundedness and finiteness of our personal lives, we are forced to acknowledge that we are not solitary individuals. The culture of narcissism, on the other hand, refuses to own this reality. It prefers to provide entertaining distractions from the truth of the human predicament. Yet in owning the reality of our woundedness, we Christians have a basis for an authentic openness to one another. Intergenerational compassion in Christian community reveals to us that despite our wounds and incompleteness, we have a powerful source of healing when we embrace the unity that is ours as the body of Christ. The mystery of the Christ life reveals the solidarity of human community.

The Church's response to the powerful mystique of narcissism is to call us to ministry. *Cosmopolitan, Esquire,* or the *New York Times Magazine* teach us how to embellish the facade of our ego so as to protract indefinitely a narrative fiction of social meaning, but the individual self as the focus of cosmetic attention and fictional invention is, after all, a pitiful sight. The radical challenge of the gospel is to see the self as "for others." It is interesting to remember Dietrich Bonhoeffer's habit of referring to Jesus as "the man for others." Ministry, for Bonhoeffer, is integral to the understanding of Christian life.

In response to the privatization of ultimate issues, the Church has increasingly seen the powerful connection between the corporal works of mercy and the presence of God in society. In the last two decades, all the Christian Churches have become more vocal in expressing their concern for social justice. The fate of the human community and the fate of the earth concern us as Christians precisely because we believe that grace does become visible in social structures. Perhaps the greatest heresy of the respectable religion of our Victorian ancestors was their expectation that the grace that sanctified them and prepared an eternal redemption for them had nothing to do with the ordinary world and had no right to be visible in ordinary experience.

The illness of a world flawed by late Enlightenment fallacies needs that response of care which is the revelation of Church as a community of whole people, called to ministry in order to make visible saving grace. It would be tedious to try to point out all the ways that we have begun to elaborate such a response in recent decades. But clearly "ministry" has become the dominant theme in pastoral theology. What kind of persons, then, are able to act in the name of the Church in such a responsive way?

HUMAN DEVELOPMENT AND GENERATIVITY

A certain level of social and psychological strength is needed on the part of ministers in order to offer apt material for the work of grace in the Church community. The work of Piaget, Erikson, and Levinsor, of pastoral theologians like Don Browning and James Fowler, reflects a concern for human development issues.[4] Fundamentally this literature makes two points: First, particular kinds of human strength are acquired at certain moments of life. Erikson, for example, sees the capacity to trust and cooperate develop in fundamental ways in childhood. Piaget has studied the way in which the capacity for creative thinking develops in adolescence. Second, such forms of human development are the raw material for grace and ministry. In Catholic theology we have the familiar axiom "grace builds on nature." Conversely, the lack of natural or human development becomes an impediment to the proper functioning of God's grace in the minister and in the community. Such a claim seems confirmed in the light of contemporary religious psychology.

The kind of ministry that is most essential for this dramatic moment in the development of the Church's life is a ministry of generativity. Our moment is one of dramatic transition. We know with reliable conviction that our institutions will have to change. The pool of candidates for male, celibate, life-time, ordained ministry is drying up. As Dean Hoge's 1987 study, *The Future of Catholic Leadership*, repeatedly underlines, even significant improvement in the number of candidates for the seminary will still leave the Church with a scenario of unprecedented change in ministerial expectations.[5] Future priests will need to concentrate on empowering non-ordained co-workers. They will need to be constantly preoccupied with identifying, educating, and advancing the roles of a new generation of lay pastoral ministers. Such leadership flows from the developmental maturity called generativity.

Erikson assigns his category of generativity to the moment of adult maturing when persons turn beyond the projects of their own ego development and beyond their own most self-preoccupied projects. Since his normative idea of growth passes through individual adult achievement, courtship and marriage, and the raising of a family, his fundamental notion of generativity deals with moving beyond family concerns to the wider social community. He explicitly acknowledges that there is such a thing as celibate generativity. But married or not, all of us at some point are called to achieve a wider perspective for our work or ministry, a perspective concerned with the whole community and the growth in skills of a younger generation.

When we look at the problems of the social order cited above, what becomes evident is that generative ministers and life-enhancing ministries can respond in significant ways. What are some qualities of generativity?

GENERATIVE MINISTRY

Generative ministers are able to envisage projects beyond their own ego-concerns. The phrase "ego trip" refers to the way in which people make their own work or community actions adjectives of their own self and their own reputation. This is normal to some degree, but it is also something that we must move beyond. The ego trip leaves the individual at the center of things, and thus very often limits the role allowed to those who assist in the project. The Church is a believing assembly expressing itself as a community. Therefore, the ministerial ego trip, or egocentric expression of ministry, is a fundamental deformation of the Church's self-understanding.

Thomas Szasz described two forms of leadership: leadership for dependence and leadership for independence—and we must clearly choose between one or the other.[6] This is an inescapable reality of our time and our new age. In the past, leaders very often helped communities by very directive forms of engagement. Now it is clear that the fundamental task of a religious leader is to lead the community to accept the awesome mystery that each one of us, baptized in Christ, is called to participate in the making of God's kingdom. The key dynamic in leadership for independence is participation.

Jean Piaget made a distinction between dependency and autonomy relationships. In dependency relations, someone is on top—with a superior authority—and others find themselves on a lower rank of obedient response. There is a whole emotional or moral ecology (to coin a metaphor) that goes along with dependency relations. Hierarchy, classical solutions, closed issues, and authoritarian attitudes are part and parcel of dependency relations. By contrast, in leadership by autonomy, the leader strives as far as possible to develop peer relations among the members of the community. In the last twenty-five years we have elucidated such leadership terms as facilitator, moderator, animator. All of these terms are ways of expressing the fundamental goal of the leader: to foster participation.

Such a leader keeps a loose grasp on the direction of the community. Ministers have to know the members of the community and their potential. Plans that may be theoretically ideal but a poor match for the capacities of this particular group of people will not foster participation. Prizing past solutions or some other community's activities will turn off and alienate potential participants. Aiding an assembly to see its possibilities and choose a life of its own, on the other hand, will generate both numbers and enthusiasm.

The key issue centers on how a pastoral leader facilitates healing, transformation, and spiritual growth by inviting others into the dynamics of peer cooperation. The integrity of the minister is quite important for this kind of leadership. The priest or non-ordained Catholic minister must somehow be able to respect the spiritual condition and pastoral capacity of the people with whom he or she works. A collaborative and cooperative spirit, seeking to affirm the assistance and participation of the whole community, depends upon the human development of the ministers. Piaget's autonomy, with its spirit of peer respect for equal colleagues, is a developmental achievement required for enabling leadership.

In summary, for our world today, sickened by competition and individualism, empowerment is healing. A pastoral community, rooted in the action of the Holy Spirit of God, is a therapeutic community. As stated above, we do not exist as a people of God in a neutral context. Rather, we exist in a corrosive context, one debilitated by individualism, narcissism, and privatization. To address these ills we must invite people beyond the ego-focused condition of the world around them. To invite people into the profound exchange of mutual assistance that makes their lives a visible sign of Church, the body of Christ, is both human development and sacramental transformation.

MODERN DYSFUNCTIONS AND MINISTRIES

Within the contemporary American Church, we find many people burdened with loneliness and aimlessness, overload and stagnation, depression, lethargy, and seduction by a corrupting secularism. Too often our response to these heavy burdens of spiritual dysfunction has been formalism or legalism; the Church goes about its business in an impersonal way. What a contrast to the situation of need and genuine response, hurt and appropriate help, developmental disabilities and pastoral care. But for the Church to be able to respond to the pastoral needs of hurting people, its ministers must possess both spiritual integrity and a sacramental focus with the power to transform the ordinary.

A key dysfunction within our contemporary society is loneliness. Feelings of pain, emptiness, and worthlessness often accompany the condition of being an outsider. Our highly technical and highly competitive society maximizes the possibility that many people will feel out of place, disjointed, or unproductive. Such a condition produces not only a pained existence for the individual, but also a wound for the Church community. The emotionally withdrawn among us become inert members of the parish community.

Social and emotional withdrawal also block the leaven of the gospel. New Testament affirmations of God's unconditional love, of the Christian vocation, and of the dynamic guidance of the Spirit need fertile ground to take root in human lives. Loneliness is too arid a base for gospel living. It filters out the good news and dims the vision that the Christian Church proclaims.

We have become more aware, especially in recent years, that we can respond to this condition. Both counseling and volunteer service can become dynamic remedies for the lonely. A helping relationship of deep trust can sometimes break through the emptiness and defensiveness of lonely people. Offering to the lonely the opportunity for community service often dramatically improves their sense of worth and belonging.

For decades now we have included in our youth ministry programs opportunities for service in soup kitchens, social service to the elderly, or assistance to the handicapped. In some cases, such experiences produce significant change in the social vision of young people. The young frequently give evidence of varying levels of loneliness and alienation; in volunteer service this withdrawal is addressed. The alienation of young Americans so often a result of their feeling unimportant to their busy parents and irrelevant in a highly complex society can be addressed by effective participation in ministry, no matter how simple the action. In the very act of social engagement by which they take part in caring for someone more needy, they become emotionally involved in the lives of others and affirmed for the worthiness of their own persons and for their spirit of generosity.

Volunteer service among the retired can also draw those relatively withdrawn from social interaction into useful and affirming interaction. In either case, the social experiences become the material for a more profound understanding of the gospel. The helping and the healing are substantially the same act; caring and care go together.

Another dysfunction is overload and the spirit of activism that promotes it. *Time* magazine, that diagnostic gadfly of our culture, devoted an April 1989 cover story to the overload syndrome. Americans seem driven to remain overstimulated, overgratified, and overdosed, but there are signs that the culture at large may be growing in its awareness of the dangers of such activism and of the burdens of stress and fatigue.[7]

This culture of overstimulation creates a lethal environment of compulsive overdependence on providers of superficial excitement. Conspicuous consumption crowds out disciplined evaluation of subtle quality. A crushing quantity of events crowds out possibilities for replenishing leisure. At bottom, there appears to be a fundamental ego insecurity among people who feel they need to be told what is worthwhile, fad by fad, and how to invest their life and energy.

In addition, this culture of overstimulation has a reductionistic effect on values. Everything is thrown into the same context of competing distractions. Christian symbols vie with astrology, financial investments, and high fashion as imperative resources for ego embellishment. The overall result is enervating.

What does the Christian community have to offer as an alternative to the culture of overstimulation? Has the dominant trend of drivenness dulled our sensibilities to the point that religious practice can only function as archaic superstition or quaint withdrawal? It is difficult to read the signs. There is a religious revival of sorts going on in our country. More and more air time is given to radio and television evangelists, at the same time that talk shows (which hold nothing sacred) also thrive. Religion as a personal interest focused on relieving emotional emptiness or satisfying curiosity does have a substantial clientele. TV evangelists who operate as salvation merchants appear to be selling peace of mind for the price of impassioned attachment to a fundamentalist canon of biblical texts and free will offerings to support their media costs. It is hard not to see cynicism behind the apparatus of TV evangelism. Its cultural impact strongly reinforces both social and emotional escapism.

CHRISTIAN BASE COMMUNITIES

One of the most hopeful phenomena in our world today is the appearance and growth of communities where individualism has been replaced by strong corporate life, where narcissism has been confronted and channeled into ministerial service, and where privatism has been broken down to create common energies for Christian witness. These communities are often referred to as "base communities." The first examples arose out of the desperate struggle of the poor in Latin America to find dignity and a voice in a society where they had long felt impotent. In the past fifteen to twenty years, the dynamics of solidarity of values, mutual service, and common action for the transformation of society have spread to base communities of varying kinds around the world.

In the U.S. the most common example of this is the RCIA catechumenal community. When leadership and chemistry are right, the catechumenal culture reaches out to transform the whole parish. The RCIA grew out of a conviction that adult conversion requires not just reasonable assent to creeds, but also a thorough reorientation of one's whole symbolic universe, beginning with the fundamental symbol of relations: belonging. Those who have worked with the catechumenate can doubtless verify the principle that the power of open communication generates a context thick with meaning, capable of illuminating and energizing the rites and symbols of the Church.

The base community turns upside-down long cherished popular understandings of how sacramental transformation works. Instead of sacramental consecration creating the holy for a neutral world void of holiness, Christian base community understands Eucharist as a revelation of the presence of the holy within the life of a people formed by God's Spirit. Instead of sacramental actions emphasizing the hierarchical distance between minister and people, Christian base community understands all sacred action as concelebration—a full involvement of each believer in the mystery proclaimed as a manifestation of authentic life. Instead of the focus of Christian symbols falling upon the material elements used in ritual celebration, the base community recognizes that its own response—its own converted interaction—is the focus of sacramental life. Both the style of ministry and the image of transformation are substantially reshaped within base community. The ministry is community-focused and generative. The subject of transformation is the people themselves far more than the things they touch and share.

What is pastoral care for a world that has given privileged place to individualism, competition, and privatism? It is first of all the transvaluation, the redefinition of the world itself. Not unlike the earliest days of the Christian Church, at a time when it existed as an outlawed phenomenon in a declining Roman world, the local Church today is first of all a manifestly alternative existence within the prevailing culture. Its focus is not centrally upon the egocentric concerns of individuals. Its focus is rather upon the revelation of a world in which people of diverse ages, backgrounds, status, and interests become at a radical level "one body, one Spirit in Christ."

There are an abundance of opportunities for the parish or local Church to redefine itself as Christ's people. Generative ministry is marked by certain characteristics of ritual action. First, ritual must be expressive of peer relation. Ministers must understand that the solidarity of faith and spirit that they share with their people is incomparably more important than any hierarchical title of dignity or position that they hold as leaders. Further, ritual, as far as possible, should involve the entire assembly physically in the execution of the rites. We excuse ourselves too easily from such universal involvement of the people, since ritual action is where transformation most naturally takes place.

Second, ritual action has a powerful capacity to form a communal identity. The voices of a people joined in song and common praise is a moving phenomenon. This unity is deepened and strengthened when the people vocalize their differences of viewpoint and experience within a context of mutual belonging. The new conservatism, feminism, and specialized ethnic interests, however, are examples of forces which risk introducing a struggle for domination into the Christian assembly. Somehow the assembly must find ways to listen to this diversity and enact gestures of a yet more substantial unity. Honest cooperation alone, not a struggle for domination, will produce visible signs of the "one Spirit who is at work in all" (1 Cor 12:6).

Third, ritual that is generative has the capacity to create an environment attuned to numinosity. Within the past hundred years, the word "numinosity" has been used to evoke the quality of a space or an attitude suffused with the presence of the divine. The risk for a high, formal Church like Roman Catholicism is to presuppose that church buildings, art, and ritual texts produce *ipso facto* (*ex opere operato*) a sense of God's presence, while, in fact, divine love is symbolized most strongly by genuine mutual engagement that allows access to and contact with the icons of the holy. A manifest reverence symbolized in the interactions of ordinary life will bring an even greater density of meaning to the Eucharistic table. As a person progressively awakens to the awesome mystery of God's presence in all things, she or he has a far better chance of meeting God in the conventional symbols of the Christian sacraments than do those who imagine that these sacraments alone are the vehicles of grace in the world.

There are many moments when these dynamics of ritual can be applied. The meetings of leadership groups will fall by force of habit into the rituals of secular management unless the community intentionally orients its interaction toward peer relation, communal identity, and attention to the numinous. Retreats are occasions where communities have the right time and space to improvise and create new ritual actions. Likewise, spiritual direction and pastoral counselling are occasions for spontaneous ritual expression. Some very few dioceses and parishes in this country have celebrated pastoral conventions in which the achievements of the people are honored and goals for the future set and accepted. May there be many, many more examples of such prophetic ritual solidarity.

This refocusing or transvaluation of the world will require generativity on the part of the leaders of the community. We are far from this realization of Church in most of our parishes. Most Catholics are only slowly awakening to the seriousness of the priest shortage. The dominant response of Church administrators has been a reluctant, grudging accommodation to priestless Sundays. The genuine need is elsewhere. We need communities that live by the images of the gospel, that own their responsibility to build a world governed by those images, and that recognize their capacity to draw from this shared life a witness to a living gospel for a new century.

Generativity is the gift of empowerment. In the emerging Church that faces us, empowerment will be both healing and engaging. Before individual ritual moments can take on their numinous and sacramental significance, the relational structure of the community must be made more authentic and empowering. It will take years of generative ministry to assure the development of such communities.

CONCLUSION

In a narcissitic culture, examples of Christian value-based communities will have an increasingly important role to play. St. Thomas used the axiom *de esse ad posse valet illatio*: one can argue from the existence of a phenomenon that it is possible for it to be repeated or replicated. When I celebrated with the community of San Egidio at Pentecost, I thought of the healing energy that was mediated by their liturgy and their hospitality. It is a community that really does think of itself as ecclesial: the links of hospitality are obvious; their investment in a numinous liturgy expresses mutual joy in the presence of the Lord; the apostolic outreach of the community is organic to its identity. In the weeks before I finally visited San Egidio, I heard persons of vastly different orientation speak of the community with appreciation and excitement. San Egidio transcends categories of liberal/conservative, high Church/low Church, institutional/servant Church. Something radical has been touched and liberated in this base community that meets so many very different people precisely at the level of their deepest need.

Paul J. Philibert, O.P.

Pastoral care in our day must begin with this kind of radical encounter. Isolated ritual gestures may mediate God's healing love and bring solace and support to broken people within a more diffuse or scattered Church assembly. But the fundamental ill and the fundamental hunger of our contemporaries is for a transvalued life; a life lived in fellowship on a journey to sacramental incandescence. If and when we can live contemplation, prayer, and mutual service with convincing intensity, we will find ourselves mutually enabling and delighting one another in the Spirit of Christ. Generative ministers will lead the way. Such persons are those who will act in the power of the realized Christian community even before the fullness of that community has been made palpable. How marvelous that there are lanterns of hope like the community of San Egidio in Trastevere to challenge our imagination and convince us of the possibility. Wholeness is healing.

NOTES

1. See Christopher Lasch, *The Culture of Narcissism: American Life in an Age of Diminishing Expectations* (New York: Warner Books, 1989); *The Minimal Self: Psychic Survival in Troubled Times* (New York: W. W. Norton, 1984); Robert N. Bellah et al., *Habits of the Heart: Individualism and Commitment in American Life* (Berkeley: University of California Press, 1985); Richard J. Bernstein, *Beyond Objectivism and Relativism: Science, Hermeneutics, and Praxis* (Philadelphia: University of Pennsylvania Press, 1983).
2. The individualism of our social order is based precisely upon a theory of rights. A philosophy of rights takes the individual person in isolation as the subject of reflection. Without specifically denying relations or community, a philosophy of rights nonetheless presupposes that the claims to property, opportunity, or privilege are based on the dignity of the individual as a person. While I do not deny the general conclusions of such a philosophy, it is a very different thing to arrive at these same conclusions from a perspective of a common inheritance of rational nature, graced destiny, and communal celebration of the vision of what is authentically human. In recent years, the claims of the underprivileged for employment, for educational opportunities, and for voice within the political process have been heard less commonly within the public arena, shaped by a philosophy of rights, than within the Church.

   At the same time, it is very important to note that our ability to raise critical social questions is the fruit of Enlightenment thinking. In no way would we be wise to imagine that we might return to a pre-Enlightenment social order.

3. Aquinas's moral teaching imagines that the emotions are meant to be guided by reason through the action of prudence and that the goal of the moral virtues is for the emotions to find balanced, appropriate pleasure in the objects that attract them. See, e.g., *Summa Theologiae* 1a2ae, q. 65, a. 1, ad 3, and 1a2Ae, q. 59, a. 3c. W. D. Hughes, ed., *Virtue,* vol. 23 (New York: McGraw-Hill, 1969) 183, 89–90.

4. For theological reflection upon Piaget and Erikson, see Walter E. Conn, *Conscience: Development and Self-Transcendence* (Birmingham: Religious Education Press, 1981); Daniel J. Levinson et al., *Seasons of a Man's Life* (New York: Knopf, 1978); James W. Fowler, *Stages of Faith: The Psychology of Human Development and the Quest for Meaning* (San Francisco: Harper & Row, 1981); Don Browning, *Religious Ethics and Pastoral Care* (Philadelphia: Fortress, 1983).

5. Dean Hoge, *The Future of Catholic Leadership: Responses to the Priest Shortage* (Kansas City: Sheed & Ward, 1987).

6. Thomas Szasz, *The Second Sin* (Garden City, N.Y.: Anchor Press, 1973).

7. Nancy Gibbs, *Time* (April 24, 1989) 59: "Experts tracking the cause and effect are coming to see how progress has carried hidden costs. 'Technology is increasing the heartbeat,' says Manhattan architect James Trunzo, who designs 'automated environments.' 'We are inundated with information. The mind can't handle it all.'. . . In business especially, the world financial market almost never closes, so why should the heavy little eyes of an ambitious baby banker? 'There is now a new supercomputer that operates at a trillionth of a second,' says Robert Schrank, a management consultant in New York City. 'What's a trillionth of a second? Time is being eaten up by all these new inventions. Even leisure is done on schedule.'"

Gilbert Ostdiek, O.F.M.

Ritual Process and the Human Journey

INTRODUCTION

The issue I propose to explore in this paper is a simple one. In academic language, one may speak of the parallels between sacramental process and human experience. Pastoral theologians may choose to examine ritual process and human journey.

Quite simply, the familiar question is this: How is the Christian story *my* story, *my* journey?

If, as Paul writes, Christ is the "last Adam" (1 Cor 15:45) in whom we are all summed up, is he not our "everyone"? Is his story not the master-story for us all? Can we not tell and enact his story in the Christian assembly in such a way that we know it is ours?

We can share stories of times when we felt disconnected from what the liturgy proclaimed and enacted, or of other times, in celebrations great or small, when word and gesture truly evoked a sense of the holiness of our lives in God's presence. What is important about the stories is not their personal details or what we may have gained from the experience, but rather that we have such experiences in common. They disclose rather pointedly that we are a story-people. We love to hear our life journeys told in these moments of ritual story-telling. We are endowed with a remarkable ability to resonate with a single shared story across the differences of our individual lives and to sense the common human journey which lies within these stories.

There is an innate hunger for this recognition that we are on a life journey and that we have a story to tell. In a study that explores the personal religious journeys of people and how these relate to the institutional life of the Church, Jean Haldane reports:

> The private nature of the journey is partly responsible for the fact that it appears to "occur on the side" in the church. It is not talked about there. There is a veritable "conspiracy of silence" about it. It is peripheral to, not parallel with the church. It is simply there, untapped and unrecognized, an underground of experience that is the personal context for what happens to each person in the church.

> Another fact that discourages people from talking about the religious journey is that no one in the church ever asks about their personal faith and practice.

Several pages later Haldane concludes: "I am struck by the fact that the church does seem to be concerned with telling and not with listening."[1]

Another example serves to elucidate this point. Recently I had occasion to collaborate with Dr. Herbert Anderson from the pastoral department at Catholic Theological Union, Chicago, in teaching a seminar on worship and pastoral care.[2] One of our goals was to engage the students in exploring parallels between sacramental process and human process. As we listened to the accounts and reflections of the students, we found our working assumption confirmed again and again: There are far more connections between ritual process and life journey than we normally make in our academic disciplines.

Story and journey are images that suggest an experiential, reflective tone regarding the vital connection between ritual and pastoral care. The images are rich and ambiguous, appropriate descriptions for both ritual and pastoral care. Pastoral care is predicated on journeying with others and helping them to voice their story. As one writer observed, the perennial strategy of the liturgy is, "gather the folks, tell the story, break the bread."[3]

In the first two parts of this essay, I will explore the question: what human experience, what human dynamic is implied in the celebration of a sacrament? In part three I will raise a second question: if in celebrating our rituals we take human experience seriously, what effect will this have on ritual and pastoral care?

TWO EARLY COMMUNITY STORIES

Two stories from the experience of the early Christian community provide insight into the human dynamics of sacraments. These stories are chosen because they recount the "first" sacramental celebrations of the community. *Emmaus* (Luke 24:13-35)

Mark's Gospel contains a very brief version of this story. We read: "Later on, as two of them were walking along on their way to the country, he was revealed to them completely changed in appearance. These men retraced their steps and announced the good news to the others"(16:12-13). Two simple verses express the point of all the appearance stories: recognition of the Risen Lord and continued mission in his name.

Why has Luke so carefully crafted the story, and with such detail? And why is his version such a perennial favorite? Can it be that from the very beginning we have all recognized in the Lucan account something of our own journey of faith? "Journeying in faith" is precisely the point of the Emmaus story and of the stories that precede and follow it in chapter 24. In each of these three resurrection stories Luke recounts a journey of faith. Little by little the disciples are led farther out from Jerusalem and deeper into the experience of Easter faith and the mission it entails. When we read the passage with attention to their interior experience, the journeying in faith becomes clear.

The road the disciples walk leads not just to Emmaus, but away from Jerusalem, away from the band of disciples, away from the hopes that had brought them there. The stranger's innocent question, "What are you discussing?" brings to the surface the distress they feel (24:17) and their need to recount once again all "the things that went on there these past few days" (24:19). Deep disillusionment is palpable in their words as they tell the story: "We were hoping . . ." (24:21). Reflecting on the story at this point, one commentator notes:

> They speak of Jesus and of their own hopes in the past tense. . . . The disciples' story is told in the language of failure, disappointment and hurt bewilderment. They tell the story from the point of view of its failure, and if people are affected by the significant stories they tell, then the disciples see themselves in terms of their story: they are ex-followers of a prophet, with left-over lives, and nowhere to go but away.[4]

Once their bitter story has exhausted itself, the stranger retells it so that it ends not in failure, but in glory. "Did not the Messiah have to undergo all this so as to enter into his glory?" (24:27). The words he uses are familiar, but the meaning is new. So compelling is his retelling of the story that their hearts are transformed, the cold heaviness within them replaced with a warmth they cannot yet name. The "arsonist of the heart," to use John Shea's image,[5] has done his work. Hosting their hurt, he frees them to think beyond themselves and beyond what they had understood by the recent experiences in Jerusalem. They repay his hospitality with an invitation of their own: "Stay with us" (24:29). But the cycle of hospitality is not over. He assumes the role of host, leading them in the ritual of the breaking of the bread. "With that their eyes were opened and they recognized him" (24:31).

The table rite marks a moment of completion and transformation in their journey. The geographic journey from Jerusalem to Emmaus simply images their inner journey of coming to believe. The journey began long before the two came to Jerusalem. A fragile "little faith" (24:25) had been enkindled in them as they first came to know this Jesus of Nazareth and to see in him "a prophet powerful in word and deed in the eyes of God and all the people" (24:19). But that dawning faith too soon knew its own dark night in the traumatic events of the week in Jerusalem. Thus their journey turned into the flight that left Jesus a stranger to them, their faith shattered, and their hopes empty and hollow. They thought they had nowhere to go but away. Under the deft care of the stranger, what seemed to be the loss of everything is transformed into the final fulfillment of their quest. The meaning of their experience is broken open and transformed as the story is retold; in the moment of the table rite they come to full Easter faith, recognizing the stranger as "the Lord" (24:34) and themselves as believing disciples. They have reached the goal of their inner journey. They rise then from the table and immediately set out on a return journey to the disciples in Jerusalem, gripped by their new story and consumed with the mission to tell the others "what had happened on the road and how they had come to know him in the breaking of the bread" (24:35).

In contemporary terms, the story embraces a marvelous flow from pastoral encounter to catechesis, from catechesis to table ritual, from ritual to mission. Nevertheless, while such terms may be helpful for our purposes, the language is still far too objective and extrinsic. Without doubt an inner human dynamic lies within this experience of the "first Eucharist" in the early community. For the two disciples it has been an inner journey to Easter faith, and the Lord has been the perfect companion on that journey, exemplifying in himself the integration of pastoral care and ritualizing which we seek to recover. The account provides the beginning of an answer.

Pentecost (Acts 2:1-41). But the question still remains: what human experience, what human dynamic is implied in the celebration of a sacrament? The story of Pentecost, which recounts the "first celebration of Christian initiation," also offers us the beginnings of an answer. Though the inner journey to faith by the first converts is more veiled, some traces do remain. The story is quickly told.

The bystanders "were dumbfounded and could make nothing at all" (2:12) of what they had witnessed. For the most part, they experienced only an idle curiosity. "What does this mean?" (2:12), they ask. Their question invites a "kerygmatic moment"[6] in which Peter cites prophet and psalm to cast a different light on what they have experienced. They are "deeply shaken" (RSV: "cut to the heart") by what they have heard. Mere curiosity is no longer enough: they now have a new, personal question: "What are we to do, brothers?" (2:37). In asking that question they have reached a first "threshold" on their journey to faith; they have moved from a curiosity of the mind to a searching of their hearts and lives. (Note, too, that they have already begun to identify themselves with the community by their manner of address.)

This new question leads into a "catechetical moment" during which they listen, probably over an extended period of time, to Peter's arguments and exhortations to save themselves "from this generation" (2:40). The curiosity-seekers turned heart-searchers now cross a second "threshold" almost unnoted in the text. The passage simply describes them as "those who accepted his message" (2:41). They have come to full faith that Jesus is "both Lord and Messiah" (2:36); they are ready to take their place among the community of disciples.[7]

The story of this "first initiation" quickly draws to a close. They undergo a ritual bath and are "added [to the community] that day" (2:41). From curiosity to heart-searching to believing, their lives have been changed and they have entered with the community upon the new way of living summarized in the final lines of the story (2:42-47).

From these two "first sacrament" stories we can already discern some of the elements needed to sketch the relation between sacrament and human experience. The participants in each story experience a series of events. But it is only as they live into these events and try to search out their meaning that they "own" the experience; it is not simply something that happens to them. The question, "What are we to do?", is the moment of awakening.

Ritual Process and the Human Journey

There are also moments of transformation, when the meaning of the experience is seen in a radically new light. When the bread is broken, eyes open in recognition and hearts are sensitized to the burning within.

These moments, however, do not stand alone. The meaning of the experience which lies inside the events of each story unfolds in a dynamic process. The breaking of bread and the ritual bath are not isolated events; they come only at the end of a journey in faith and serve to sum up and mark the journey already accomplished. First comes the experience; then, the retelling and interpretation; finally, the sacramental moment. In turn, the sacramental rituals open onto a further journey still to be made; they lead the participants back into community life and mission. Sacraments, then, are ritual events within a process; they serve to mark a special moment of completion, transformation and new beginning.

But the stories reveal that there are other significant moments or thresholds in the process as well, moments when the transformation of the experience and the disclosure of its meaning are carried one step further. Peter's preaching, for example, evokes a new question and a moment of decision. These moments, too, need to be named and marked, perhaps through a series of ritual events woven into a larger ritual process to frame the journey. These rituals work together to disclose that the process is both human and holy, one of coming to full human stature as believers, as covenant partners with God. Thus there is an overlay of human process and sacramental process.

Finally, these stories also suggest that sacraments are never private transactions between an individual and God. The rituals and the processes they mark involve the community of believers as well; all who are disciples follow Jesus on the way together.

SACRAMENT AND JOURNEY

These preliminary insights that suggest a necessary connection between human experience and human process on the one hand and sacramental process on the other must now be tested and developed vis-à-vis sacramental theory and practice. The reflections that follow will develop from a series of five statements, with sample illustrations from various sacraments. The Rite of Christian Initiation of Adults (RCIA) is the constant paradigm.[8]

It is useful at the outset to make some preliminary distinctions.

First, "raw experience" is not "lived experience."[9] There is a difference, for example, between fixing a snack and preparing a special meal for a close friend. "Raw experience" (fixing a snack) is something we simply go through; it has no special meaning for us. It becomes "lived experience" (preparing a special meal) when we reflect on what it means, naming it and gradually integrating it into the story of our lives. Only then does the experience attain full human significance.

Second, outer event and inner experience[10] are also distinct, yet related. The relationship is a symbolic one. Consider a handshake or a hug. Inner meaning is lived out in the external event, and that event evokes, shapes, and expresses the meaning within. This outer/inner dynamic holds not only for the individual moments of the experience, but also for the larger sequences in our lives. For example, inner journeys often seek expression in, or are occasioned by, an outer, physical journey. And when we need to tell our inner experience, the story of a journey is often the form we choose.[11] The Emmaus story illustrates well this connection.

1. *Sacramental events are part of a larger ritual process.* The ritual event we call a sacrament is not an isolated event; it is part of a longer ritual process, one of a series of ritual events. This is clear in the RCIA, where three major rituals, the rite of acceptance into the catechumenate, the rite of election, and sacramental initiation, form a series of ritual bridges marking the different periods of the initiatory process.

The liturgical tradition provides additional evidence for the existence of ritual process. The ancient rite of penance, patterned on the catechumenate, included a rite of entry into the order of penitents, a time of penance, and a rite of reconciliation. The candidate for holy orders passed through a number of ritual stages, including tonsure and a series of "minor" and "major" orders. And in the history of marriage, there are three rival claimants for the title of being the sacramental moment: betrothal, wedding, and consummation. In retrospect these theories can be interpreted as tradition's way of identifying the significant moments in an unfolding process.[12] Each in fact generated its own form of liturgical ritual. Sacramental events have been and continue to be embedded in larger ritual processes.

2. *There is a correlation between ritual process and human process.*

The sacramental rites themselves manifest this correlation. My premise is that sacraments are symbolic ritual actions that derive their meaning not only from their Christian origins and history, but from human symbolic usage as well.

For example, the human root of baptism is the act of bathing. But note that it is not a bathing of oneself, but being bathed by someone else who represents the group. There are many human meanings embedded in that simple act of bathing, and they are rooted in the way water envelops us. Bathing means many things: cleansing and refreshment in waters which speak on a deeper level of birth and death; the group's care to bring others to birth and to sustain their life in the face of death; taking those bathed into our arms and our care; and simply coming to belong, being entrusted, in body and spirit, to the group and to each other. If such meanings are truly symbolized in bathing, they cannot be constricted to one moment; they spill over and we commit ourselves to live them for a lifetime. Bathing someone symbolizes an ongoing process of incorporation, belonging, and generativity.

The human ritual underlying the Eucharist, the sharing of food and drink, provides another example. Bread and wine each speak in their own way of human work and life; of unrelenting hunger and daily sustenance; of unsatisfied thirst and festive celebration; of those who share food and life and of those who want; of the community that is and the community that ought to be. What is ritualized in table sharing is not just the exchange of food and drink, but the gift of our lives, our very selves. Like bread, life is not one's own possession; it is ours in common, to be broken and given. By this simple exchange of food we are caught in a lasting web of mutual indebtedness and interdependence, we owe our lives and ourselves to one another.[13] Every time we share food, we ratify a life-pact with our table companions (literally those who eat bread together) and we proclaim that no one ought to be excluded from the circle and table of life.

It is the same with the other sacramental rites. The exchange of marital vows by a couple expresses far more than a momentary joining of hands and hearts; it gathers up and symbolizes the long human process of becoming a couple. The element of the entrance rite (in the marriage ceremony) that causes us so many pastoral problems, the parental act of "giving" a child to be married, points to another, often neglected process, that of leaving parents and home.[14] In the sacrament of penance the ritual exchange of apology and pardon focuses a far longer process of reconciliation.[15] Anointing the sick with oil makes this act of healing and human caring a ritual action against the isolation[16] set in motion by the experience of sickness and debility; it makes sense only in the context of a human process of constant caring for those in our midst who are sick.

In terms of the basic actions described above, sacramental rituals are human rituals. They bring with them the kinds of human meaning embodied in the gestures and the words we speak as we perform them. But is the meaning only human?

3. *Sacramental ritualization names the human process a saving process.* In a sacramental rite human actions with human meaning, like bathing, are performed, but with a difference. A sense of sacredness, a sense of God's presence pervades the action; words of prayer and Scripture interpret what the action means. The liturgy of the Word and the liturgical prayers that accompany the sacramental action both tell us that the experience we ritualize in a sacrament is not just a human experience, but an experience of God's presence and action in our lives.

Recall the earlier examples. We bathe someone in the name of the Lord Jesus, or in the name of the Trinity. These words are a kind of shorthand. The full biblical story of baptism which we hear in the readings speaks of how, by God's doing, someone plunged into those waters dies to sin and is born again into a people who can live in a new way. The baptismal formula sums up this story and proclaims that God has transformed our ritual bathing to bring us to new life beyond the death of sin and to lead us into covenant community and belonging. In the Eucharist the institution account accompanies the sharing of bread. That account sums up how God, in the table practice first of the Jews and then of Jesus, has infused our human food-sharing with a new, covenantal meaning. Christian Eucharist is a retelling and a reenacting of the Lord's table presence and self-gift for the life of the world; it is a ratification of our pledge to live out that same pattern of service.

In one and the same breath, sacramental symbols speak a meaning that is both human and saving. If the human meaning of a ritual is to be found not only in the ritual moment but also in life, must the same be said for the saving meaning? Must sacrament then be extended beyond the moment of ritual to all of human life? One can argue, as Karl Rahner does, that the world is graced permanently at its core.[17] The drama of God's self-offering and of our human response (which reached its high point in Jesus) lies at the heart of history and constitutes a "liturgy of the world." Wherever and whenever human beings enter into the self-surrender of Jesus, they take part in that liturgy of the world. The liturgy of the Church, in the more usual sense, expresses and clarifies that larger liturgy which lies hidden in our lives. Sacramental symbols speak not only of this liturgical moment of God's presence and grace, but of the journey that has brought us this far under God's gracious but hidden guidance. The sacramental event rehearses that human journey and names it God's calling and God's grace to us. A sacrament, then, is not just an event. It is a moment within a fuller ritual process that is at once both human and saving. That is, the salvation God offers is incarnated in the very words and actions of the sacramental celebration.

4. *The sacramental process is a growing one with many significant moments.* There is a rhythm, an ebb and flow in a process. There are times when life seems uneventful. There are also turning points, critical moments when something that has been must end and something new must begin. Such moments of transition are significant because they are the threshold, the passageway from one phase of the journey into another, as in the initiation at Pentecost. These transitions may not be recognized at the time, like the "burning hearts" in the Emmaus story. When they are recognized, however, we feel a need to name them in some fashion, often in a ritualized story or gesture.

Such a pattern of growth times and marker events is woven into the RCIA process. These are familiar and need not be listed here. It suffices to note how the process unfolds. Those who begin to experience faith and conversion are guided step by step through successive periods in which that experience is named, nurtured, intensified, and prolonged. At the points of intersection, the RCIA places rituals that act as bridges, summing up what has gone before and opening into the period that follows.

One can see in the rites of election and initiation (and the period which they frame) the sacramental transformation of the process most clearly at work. During the time of the catechumenate proper, the catechumens are apprentices in the midst of the community, learning by doing. They participate fully in the life of the community through catechesis, liturgy, fellowship, and service (RCIA 75).[18] When the catechumens have matured in faith and conversion, they are chosen by the church to go on to sacramental initiation. The rite of election is truly a "focal point" (RCIA 121). In this rite the names of the catechumens are enrolled among the people of God. The rite is called *election* "because the acceptance made by the Church is founded on the election by God, in whose name the Church acts" (RCIA 119). In addition, this ritual is meant to transform the perspective of the catechumens. The long journey in which they and the community have invested so much effort is now seen to have been God's call, God's doing from the very beginning. With transformed perspective, the catechumens move directly into the Lenten season. Lent becomes for them a time of recollection and enlightenment, a time to relive and retell their conversion story in the light of God's election. It is a time of purification, a time to let God's gracious call permeate them and prepare them for the sacramental rites which will proclaim publicly their belonging to God and to the community. Building on this heightened sense of God's presence and gracious working in their lives, the Easter sacraments can, by God's transformative power, set a final seal on the faith journey the catechumens have experienced.

My intention here is not to suggest that this unfolding pattern of periods and ritual events will fit every sacrament exactly, but only that it offers us new pastoral insight into the sacramental process. The way in which the RCIA respects the growing, developing character of the journey to faith and invites and nurtures the transformation of that experience at significant moments can serve as a model for every sacrament.

5. *The sacramental process is a communal process.* The RCIA leaves no doubt that initiation is a communal process. Adult initiation is a gradual process that takes place "within the community," whose members are called upon to give an example "by joining the catechumens in reflecting on the value of the paschal mystery and by renewing their own conversion" (RCIA 4). In other words, the journey of faith and conversion the catechumens will make is

one that has been and must continue to be made by the community at large. Catechumens learn to walk the way by accompanying the other disciples who also walk it. Because the journey is one, those who walk it are one community.[19] When they gather in liturgy to mark that journey, they witness to a common story, common values, and shared hopes for the future.[20] Or as someone has put it more simply, "Sacraments don't just happen to the recipients; they happen to all of us."

The RCIA also envisions that the whole Christian community and a variety of individuals within it are called to minister to the catechumens. This resonates with systems theory which sees ritual as engaging the interaction and relationships not just of a few members, but of the entire group.[21] In a real sense, even though one minister pours the water, the entire community is a baptizing community, a generative community. The catechumens themselves exercise a prophetic ministry toward the community. Perhaps one of the most graphic moments of this ministry occurs when they are dismissed from the Lenten Sunday assembly; their departure calls those who remain for the Eucharist to undertake their own Lenten journey of renewal.

These reflections on the relation between sacramental process, human process, and sacramental celebration point to the absolute need to recover the connection between ritual and pastoral care. The reason is both compelling and simple: serving the people of God in their spiritual journeys is our common concern.

RITUAL AND PASTORAL CARE

It remains now to explore briefly some aspects of a possible new relationship between ritual and pastoral care. I will do this under the rubric of the second question I posed above. If in celebrating our rituals we take human experience seriously, what can happen to ritual and pastoral care? What follows are some of my dreams, and a few fears as well.

My first dream is that liturgy may become much more serious about story and narrative in a number of ways.[22] The communicative quality of the readings will be taken for granted. Homilies will be prepared in dialogue with those participating in the liturgy and delivered by those most credible to the community. This will hold in a special way for those rituals which mark intense personal experiences. One such instance will be marriage, when a couple entering married life begins to tell publicly a new family story (and thereby says a farewell to their families of origin). Another instance will be the rites for the dying, where effective pastoral care must include helping the dying person to bring closure to a life story. It must help the mourners at wakes and funerals to begin to shape a memory that allows for the rebuilding of existing emotional attachments and the freedom to build new ones. For example, storytelling will become a normal part of wakes.

In another vein, rites which incorporate a naming ceremony, such as the catechumenal rite of election, infant baptism, and confirmation, will be the occasion (before or during the rite) for telling why the name was chosen and what personal and family/community values and stories it sums up. Such examples illustrate how the telling of our human stories can be a prelude to the liturgical telling of the master story of Jesus. We will find ourselves and our experience told in the liturgical story; we will discover that we are not nameless individuals on private journeys, but that our experience, expressed in the same story and ritual gesture, is a shared experience and that we are a people.

My second dream is that ritual symbols will become fuller and richer. Thus, not only will Eucharistic bread more closely resemble ordinary bread; it will be broken for the assembly in a more visible manner and distributed so that we can receive together, instead of one-by-one. Ritual planning and celebration will regularly take into account the human roots and meaning of our rituals. Symbols discovered to be flawed in expressing the contemporary human experience that parallels them will be adapted pastorally. The major adaptation envisioned by Vatican II (SC 37–38) will lead to fully inculturated local liturgy. Nourished by a diet of sacramental symbols that are in touch with their human experience and rituals, people will discover anew the holiness of their lives as the place of God's dwelling and action. Cared for by such symbols and named in common story, they will find themselves confirmed and their lives joined. Such truth-telling in the rites will be an antidote to the individualism and privatization of our world.

My third dream is that sacramental ritual will blossom into true ritual process. Under the inspiration of the RCIA, we will continue to explore whether the other sacraments can be extended over time into a full sacramental process. Betrothal rites, banns, and other forms of marriage rituals will be recovered to form a series of such rituals along with the wedding. Those entering marriage will share a ritual of leave-taking with parents, and there will be a ritual for the parents of each partner to bless the new couple. We will see a greater pastoral continuity between the rites of care for the sick and dying, wakes, and funerals. There will also be rites for those experiences in our human lives that need ritual and find none (leave-takings, stillbirth,[23] entry into ministries liturgical and social, etc.)

My fourth dream is that sacramental rituals will be truly communal processes. At ritual celebrations, all will be welcomed with delight in their journey, no matter how short or how long. Neither ideals for Christian holiness nor truthfulness about human sinfulness will be denied in any ritual. Coming to know the Lord in the breaking of the bread will impel all into mission and service. Multiple ministers, collaborative and mutually supportive, will be the rule. There will be soul-friends to walk with penitents on the way to sacramental forgiveness and to help them work through the reconciling of broken relationships that remain beyond forgiveness.

I have dreams for ritual and pastoral care as well. What I hope for, above all, is that a more extended dialogue on the relation between ritual and pastoral care will begin both in parish offices and in schools of ministry. In the parishes, liturgists and pastoral care givers will work together in a more collaborative pastoral ministry. The various pastoral ministries will be less isolated; they will find greater reason to support each other and less need to bear their burdens alone. In the schools, professors in each pastoral discipline will draw insights from the others; together they will explore the intersections and common frameworks of their disciplines.[24]

I have some fears as well. Taking human experience more seriously in our celebration of the liturgy and drawing ritual and pastoral care into a closer relationship will not be without danger. The charges already levied against the renewed liturgy (that it has lost the sense of mystery and of God's transcendence) will likely increase. Broadening the concept of liturgy to speak first of the liturgy of the world and human life in the world and only then of the liturgy of the Church flies in the face of deep-seated feelings and will be resisted. The relationship between ritual and pastoral care may also run into troubled waters. The practice and meaning of sacraments may be subjected to psychologizing and reduced to stage theory. What has already been criticized as the "therapeutic use of ritual"[25] may well increase. A kind of reductionism may conclude that sacramental process is no more than human dynamics, and that a formation process can, of itself, bring about our transformation.[26] From the other side, the legitimate goals, concerns, and procedures of pastoral care may be devalued and subsumed by liturgy. Ritual may, in fact, come to occupy the position it has been assigned in the minds of some, a mechanism to repress growth-producing tensions or a magic placebo administered to avoid the hard work of pastoral care.

CONCLUSION

I have seen many signs that something new is happening in our lifetime. Liturgy is leaving the safe confines of the distant sanctuary and returning to make a home in our lives. Our hunger to tell our story and to mark our journey in ritual will not depart so easily, now that we have had a taste of how it may be satisfied. The instances of convergence we find in our ministries of companioning and enabling God's people on that journey are now too frequent to ignore. At its best, liturgy is truly a public act of caring for God's people on their journey together to the kingdom. We must make the vital connection between our ministries of ritual and pastoral care. The wholeness, the *salus*, of God's people demands it.

NOTES

1. Jean Haldane, *Religious Pilgrimage* (Washington, D.C.: The Alban Institute, 1975) 10–11, 16–17, as quoted in James Dunning, "The Stages of Initiation: I. Inquiry," in William J. Reedy (ed.), *Becoming a Catholic Christian* (New York: Sadlier, 1979) 104–5.
2. I am grateful to Herb Anderson, whose insights and support have been of great help. I also wish to acknowledge that I have drawn insights from other CTU colleagues, especially Kathleen Hughes, R.S.C.J. with whom I teach a course on sacramental process; and Anthony Gittins, C.S.Sp. an anthropologist with whom I team teach a course on cross-cultural Eucharist. Printed sources of other ideas will be identified.
3. See John Shea, *Stories of God. An Unauthorized Biography* (Chicago: The Thomas More Press, 1976) 8.
4. Denis McBride, *The Gospel of Luke. A Reflective Commentary* (Northport, N.Y.: Costello, 1982) 317–18.

5. John Shea, "The Resurrection Prayers of Magdalene, Peter, and Two Youth," in his *The Hour of the Unexpected* (Allen, Tex.: Argus Communications, 1977) 49.
6. I have adopted this schema of "moments" and "thresholds" from Michel Dujarier, *A History of the Catechumenate. The First Six Centuries* (New York: Sadlier, 1979) 19–20.
7. For further commentary on the ecclesial and developmental character of faith and repentance in Luke–Acts, see Jerome Kodell, "'The Word of God Grew,' The Ecclesial Tendency of *Lógos* in Acts (6), 7: 12,24; 19,20," *Biblica* 55 (1974) 505–19
8. Some examples of proposals that have appeared in print include the following. On reconciliation: Edward Foley, "Communal Rites of Penance: Insights and Options," in Robert J. Kennedy (ed.), *Reconciliation: The Continuing Agenda* (Collegeville, Minn.: Liturgical Press, 1987) 143–59; James Lopresti, *Penance: A Reform Proposal for the Rite,* American Essays in Liturgy, 6 (Washington, D.C.: The Pastoral Press, 1987). On marriage: Kenneth W. Stevenson, *To Join Together. The Rite of Marriage,* Studies in the Reformed Rites of the Catholic Church 5 (New York: Pueblo, 1987) 190–94. On the initiation of children (RCIC): Catherine Dooley, "Catechumenate for Children: Sharing the Gift of Faith," *The Living Light* 24 (1988) 307–17; James Dunning, "Let the Children Come to Me: Christian Initiation of Children," *Catechumenate: A Journal of Christian Initiation* 10/5 (September 1988) 2–11; 11/6 (November 1988) 22–30.
9. This distinction is taken from Tad Guzie, *The Book of Sacramental Basics* (New York: Paulist Press, 1981) 8–10.
10. I have borrowed the framework of "inner/outer" from G. van der Leeuw, *Religion in Essence and Manifestation,* vol. 2 (New York: Harper & Row, 1963) 530–34. He suggests that what psychology and phenomenology describe as the inner experience of conversion is the same as what anthropology describes as the rite of initiation.
11. See Mark Searle, "The Journey of Conversion," *Worship* 54 (1980) 35–55.
12. See Stevenson, *To Join Together,* 190–94.
13. This idea is drawn in part from Peter Farb and George Armelagos, *Consuming Passions. The Anthropology of Eating* (Boston: Houghton Mifflin, 1980), and Marcel Mauss, *The Gift. Forms and Functions of Exchange in Archaic Societies* (New York: W. W. Norton, 1967).
14. Kenneth Mitchell and Herbert Anderson, "You Must Leave before You Can Cleave: A Family Systems Approach to Premarital Pastoral Work," *Pastoral Psychology* 30 (1981) 71–88.
15. What Erving Goffman describes as "the corrective process" in human behavior shows a remarkable parallel to the sacramental process; see his *Interaction Ritual. Essays on Face-to-Face Behavior* (Garden City, N.Y.: Doubleday, 1967) 19–23.
16. Herbert Anderson and Edward Foley, "Liturgy and Pastoral Care. The Par-

able of Dying and Grieving," *New Theology Review* 1/4 (November 1988) 15–27.

17. See Karl Rahner, "On the Theology of Worship," in *Theological Investigations,* vol. 19 (New York: Crossroad, 1983) 141–49; "Considerations on the Active Role of the Person in the Sacramental Event," in *Theological Investigations,* vol. 14 (New York: Seabury, 1976) 161–84. For a commentary, see Michael Skelley, "The Liturgy of the World and the Liturgy of the Church: Karl Rahner's Idea of Worship," *Worship* 63 (1980) 112–32.

18. Paragraph references in text are to the newly revised *Rite of Christian Initiation of Adults* (Chicago: Liturgy Training Publications, 1988).

19. In his *Between Man and Man* (London: Collins, 1947), Martin Buber writes: "But community, growing community (which is all we have known so far) is the being no longer side by side but *with* one another of a multitude of persons. And this multitude, though it moves towards one goal, yet experiences everywhere a turning to, a dynamic facing of, the others, a flowing from *I* to *Thou.* Community is where community happens." Victor Turner cites this passage on the networking of I-Thou relationships, which Buber names "Essential We," to define the experience of "communitas" which can take place in moments of liminality; see Victor Turner, *The Ritual Process. Structure and Anti-Structure* (Chicago: Aldine Publishing Company, 1969) 127.

20. Victor Turner describes ritual processes, which typically occur in the third, redressive phase of a social drama, as a moment of "plural reflexivity" in which the group makes an inventory of the current state of its fundamental values and social relationships in order to assess the meaning of the present conflict and decide about the group's future; see, for example, "Images of Anti-Temporality. An Essay in the Anthropology of Experience", in his *On the Edge of the Bush. Anthropology as Experience,* ed. Edith Turner (Tucson, Ariz.: The University of Arizona Press, 1985) 232.

21. For an example of how family systems theory views the role of ritual in family life and therapy, see Evan Imber-Black, Janine Roberts, and Richard Whiting, *Rituals in Families and Family Therapy* (New York: W. W. Norton, 1988).

22. On the narrativity of liturgy, see Mark Searle, "The Narrative Quality of Christian Liturgy," *Chicago Studies* 21 (Spring 1982) 73–84.

23. See Elaine Ramshaw, "Ritual for Stillbirth: Exploring the Issues," *Worship* 62 (1988) 533–38.

24. A good beginning has been made by: Regis A. Duffy, *A Roman Catholic Theology of Pastoral Care,* Theology and Pastoral Care Series (Philadelphia: Fortress, 1983); Robert L. Kinast, *Sacramental Pastoral Care. Integrating Resources for Ministry* (New York: Pueblo, 1988); Kenneth Mitchell, "Ritual in Pastoral Care," *The Journal of Pastoral Care* 43/1 (1989) 68–77; Elaine Ramshaw, *Ritual and Pastoral Care,* Theology and Pastoral Care Series (Philadelphia: Fortress, 1987); H. P. V. Renner, "The Use of Ritual in Pasto-

ral Care," *The Journal of Pastoral Care* 23 (1979) 164–74; and William H. Willimon, *Worship as Pastoral Care* (Nashville: Abingdon, 1979).

25. See John Snow, *The Impossible Vocation. Ministry in the Mean Time* (Cambridge, Mass.: Cowley Publications, 1988) 110–30.
26. For the counter-argument, see Rosemary Haughton, *The Transformation of Man. A Study of Conversion and Community* (Paramus, N.J.: Paulist, 1967).

Kathleen Hughes, R.S.C.J.

Disciples at the Crossroads: Where Do We Go Now?

The title *Disciples at the Crossroads: Where Do We Go Now?* suggests three basic questions: 1) Who are the disciples who will lead the community into the next century? 2) As we stand at the crossroads, what are some issues facing us which may prevent us from moving forward? and 3) What are the choices that we have at this threshold moment?

WHO ARE THE DISCIPLES WHO WILL LEAD THE COMMUNITY INTO THE NEXT CENTURY?

The gospel reading for the Feast of the Apostle Barnabas states: "Jesus said to his disciples: 'As you go, make this announcement: "The reign of God is at hand!" Cure the sick, raise the dead, heal the leprous, expel demons. The gift you have received, give as a gift'" (Matt 10:7). This passage straightforwardly presents a glimpse of the work of Christian discipleship: announcing the good news, curing the sick, raising the dead, healing the leprous, expelling demons—with the caveat that God has been immensely generous to us and given so many gifts, that we, too, ought to be generous with one another: "The gift you have received, give as a gift."

But not only does the passage present a glimpse of the work of Christian discipleship; it also offers an insight into the person of the disciple. The gospel suggests that we are able to announce the reign of God in so far as we know in our deepest being that we ourselves have been cured of sickness, that we have been raised up to life when we were dead, that we have been healed of whatever has made us untouchable, that when we seemed to be possessed we have been freed—all in the immense generosity of our God. That is the gift we have received which we must give as a gift.

Knowledge of our weakness and a sense of limits are essential to anyone who would minister in the name of Jesus,[1] because only when we are willing to admit our fragility and our need for one another are we able to enter into collaborative ministry and the discipleship demanded at this moment in our history.

This stance is quite different from examining gifts and competencies and skills, important as this may be. When was the last time you sat on a search committee or talked to a personnel officer whose concerns for a potential candidate had anything to do with weakness, except perhaps, as a way to weed out undesirable applicants?

Is it not often through suffering and weakness, failure and broken dreams that persons become more whole and human? Is it not in experiences of weakness that the disciple becomes capable of understanding human needs in another and thus enabled to bring compassion to the seeker, the sick, and the penitent? Is it not essential that the one who would pray in the name of the community or interpret the word of God as a word of life be at home with the dying and rising of daily life? Are we weak enough to preside at what Jack Shea calls "the mystery which masks itself as mistake and a power which perfects itself in weakness"?[2]

Note the words about Christ, the perfect disciple, in the Letter to the Hebrews: "Because Christ himself has suffered and been tempted, he is able to help those who are tempted. . . . For we have not a high priest who is unable to sympathize with our weakness, but one who in every respect has been tempted as we are, yet without sinning. . . . He can deal compassionately with others since he himself is beset by weakness."[3]

Additional questions serve to illuminate this point:

Are we weak enough so that we cannot ward off suffering, that extraordinary forger of human depth? Have we learned to deal with confusion? to live with self-doubt? to endure anguish and fear? to tolerate frustrations? to persevere when our expectations are deflated? Have we picked ourselves up after dreams went unrealized? Have we lived with enough failure in our own lives so that we know and have come to accept what "average" really means? Do we know our sin, limits, and profound weakness and need?[4]

What kinds of demands do we place on colleagues in ministry? What kind of hours do we expect, what kind of energies, what kinds of presence? Are we intolerant of weakness in the workplace or the sanctuary? What about the dictates of culture in matters of success and failure? Do we accept the prevailing standards of a society which is highly competitive and which hides flaws as so many chinks in our social armor?

Consider the role that expectations play in what we value, in what we strive for, in what we name success, in how we measure competence in ministry. I recall the shifting expectations in my own life as a woman religious during the last twenty-five years, but I suspect that my enumeration of expectations will strike a chord in everyone.

Formation and training were so much easier and, at least in retrospect, appeared far less demanding in the closed world of twenty-five years ago. Most of us received adequate training for the work we were to undertake, though sometimes the classics major taught mathematics and the math major taught phonics. We were able to do this because of what we called, serenely, the grace of our vocation. We participated in some small measure in clerical omniscience and infallibility and rarely was our competence challenged. Expectations were clear because they were expressed in a fairly detailed rule which was supplemented by a custom book and an even more detailed order of day.

Those days are gone for good. Women religious no longer bask in the refracted light of clerical omniscience, itself a thing of the past! The expectations of rule and way of life have been supplanted by the numerous expectations of those we would serve—expectations which are overwhelming and which refer to all of us, men and women, lay and ordained. Expectations that demand we be qualified ministers (with all that that entails) also require that we be both liberal and conservative, good with children, kind to the elderly, sensitive with the disabled, and compassionate with the marginalized. We should be good at counseling, articulate in groups, adept at organization, and have something worthwhile to say about drug abuse, the defense budget, housing and hunger issues, the bishops' pastorals on peace, race relations, the economy, and the role of women in Church and society, as well as a plethora of third world concerns. We are expected to be well trained in theology and able to reflect thoughtfully on issues of contemporary concern, particularly thorny issues of morality. A variety of communication skills are demanded, an ability to listen and respond, to convene and to motivate. And in addition, we are expected to be people of faith, peace, prayer, communion, and discernment. We are expected to love the Church and to challenge it. And it wouldn't hurt if we played a musical instrument!

Have I exaggerated? Every person in this room is subject to a similar set of such expectations, real or illusory. And the list is much longer on our bad days! Expectations from others are only heightened by the expectations we place on ourselves. It is interesting how often exhaustion is interpreted as a sign of responsibility and fidelity, so that we even apologize for taking days off.

In times of rapid change, a sense of personal identity is critical. Such identity is sometimes lodged in *my* work, *my* achievement, *my* skills, *my* successes. Is not workaholism wreaking havoc on personal, familial, and communal health? Moreover, workaholism gives expression to some of the worst features of American culture: rugged individualism ("I need no one!"); competition, with its emphasis on success; and the inclination to settle conflicts by force.

When self-identity becomes one with personal achievements, I am prone to exercise a subtle violence on others: my strengths are the very things which now distance me from others who are less gifted. My developing interests may lead me to identify others as boring, unproductive, not worth my time. My talent and gifts may lead me to judge others as mediocre and simply not worth my energies.[5]

Without a profound sense of one's own weakness and essential need of others it is possible to fall into a kind of messianism, for which we may need "Messiah therapy": that is, the discovery that God so loved the world that God sent the Christ, not me, to be its Savior! Those who know their limitations, their profound weakness, their neediness, those who have experienced self-doubt and failure and deflated expectations are freer to exert moral authority, more ready to exercise integrative power with others rather than power over or against others, more aware that true discipleship at the crossroads links the exercise of any ministry with utter dependence on the God who calls us to stewardship, not domination.

WHAT ARE SOME ISSUES FACING US WHICH MAY BE PREVENTING US FROM MOVING FORWARD?

From among many, I have selected three issues which possess the potential to be profoundly divisive: 1) the vocation crisis; 2) feminism; and 3) the question of who gets to sit in the big chair when we gather for Sunday celebrations. The issues are not new; however, we have not yet asked the right questions nor appropriately located the source of our neuralgia. Further, I believe the fall-out from these issues continues to prevent us from moving beyond this juncture. We must give them a fresh hearing.

1) The "vocation crisis," I believe, is a misnomer. Our period in history is typified by an extraordinary explosion of ministries in response to the needs of our time. There are new specialized ministries to marriage, social justice, spiritual guidance, the sick, the elderly, and to those Christians who are or feel that they are marginalized or alienated in some way. An expansion of the broad ministries of healing and teaching include outreach to AIDS patients, the separated and divorced, victims of the drug culture, migrant peoples, prisoners, and those oppressed by unjust structures whether religious, economic, or political. Ministries in the Church today respond to nearly every form of human need and suffering.[6] And, quite appropriately, this breadth and diversity of ministry is manifest every time we gather for prayer. Our variety of liturgical ministries brings to public ritual expression the ministries of word, charity, and unity which should always characterize our common life in Christ.

In face of this ministry explosion, I raise the question: vocation crisis? Crisis for whom?

Surely not for the thousands of lay men and women who have heard the Council's call to a life of holiness, discipleship, and mission as a universal call, one not limited to those in an allegedly more perfect state.

Surely not for those who have heeded the United States bishops' challenge to American Catholic laity: "Everyone should painstakingly ready himself or herself personally for the apostolate, especially as an adult. For the advance of age brings with it better self-knowledge, thus enabling each person to evaluate more accurately the talent with which God has enriched each soul and to exercise more effectively those charismatic gifts which the Holy Spirit has bestowed on all for the good of others."[7]

Surely not for the Spirit of God who appears to be as active in this as in every age of the Church's life, endowing women and men with charisms of evangelisation, administration, teaching, prophecy, preaching, discernment of spirits, speaking in tongues, interpretation, miracles, healing, almsgiving, works of mercy, and apostolic works in general. We appear to be moving suspiciously close to that model of Church organization found in the New Testament where ministry was not a status or a lifestyle but, remarkably, something one did, determined by pastoral need, cultural context, and historical discernment.[8]

In fact, a glance at history confirms that particular patterns of discipleship wax and wane: the age of the desert mothers and fathers yielded to the age of monasticism which in turn was supplanted in the rise of the mendicant orders, then the apostolic orders, and then the teaching congregations. Just as forms of religious life decline when they seem no longer suited to the aspirations of the age or when they lose their sense of purpose, so, too, new forms of discipleship arise as significant social movements, often in response to dramatic social change in the church and the larger cultural and political environment. All the evidence suggests that we are on the threshold of a new age, and that is good news.[9]

It is also wise to acknowledge that the vision of discipleship and collaborative ministry in the teachings of Vatican II would have remained empty rhetoric had there not been a dramatic decline in the numbers of clergy and religious who, for too many years, were the principal pastoral agents of the Church, dispensing salvation to a passive and receptive laity. And there is the irony: the ministry explosion might never have happened except for the vocation crisis. *O felix culpa.*

The "vocation crisis" is, perhaps, applied more aptly to the many human casualties strewn at the crossroads. For it is undeniable that the public triumph of the Spirit of God at work in our world has been experienced as private loss for countless individuals who are caught between their heads and their hearts, tradition and change, dreams and disillusionment, and who are unwilling or simply unable to envision the Church in different ways or to reconceptualize their roles in a community of equal disciples.

Statisticians or systems' analysts look at changing demographics. They speak, for example, of the year 2000, noting that there will only be half the number of clergy as there are now and that there will be an equally significant decline in numbers in religious institutes. However, our concerns need to take into account the half who have stayed. A good number have been energized by change; another portion are afraid and unsure; and a significant portion are lost and frightened. For these last, the ground has shifted, the rules have changed, and the game they are playing is not the one they signed up for. To use one of Richard McBrien's observations about understated leadership, these folks are simply incapable of making change an ally.[10]

The "vocation crisis" has a human face. It is a priest now living alone in a rectory built for six, caught in the maelstrom of change, chafing at the necessity and the slowness of consultation when once his authority was unquestioned, wondering why he gets the blame and none of the praise, working too many days in a row at too many unfulfilling tasks, demoralized by the loss of respect for the priesthood, feeling always "caught in the middle" in questions of authority, identity, and competence. One priest said to me recently: "It would be easier now to be powerless than to have to share power!"

The phrase "vocation crisis" is apposite for some members of religious institutes who see their numbers decline, their median age skyrocket and their cherished institutions close; for women and men who once expressed their generativity in mentoring younger members and whose own vocational choice seemed validated by the numbers behind them in the novitiate; for women and men who have literally spent themselves in service long after the less stalwart had retired, and now fear they may not be able to retire with dignity.

The vocation crisis is our crisis, too, because the bewildered, the hurt, the fearful, the bitter are those people alongside of whom we take our places, with whom we seek to build up the body of Christ. They are our co-workers, our pastors, sometimes our bishops. They may be some of us here today. We ignore such pain at our peril.

At the beginning of this conference, Eleanor Bernstein reminded us that our theme, discipleship at the crossroads, conjures the image of the Emmaus story.[11] That story has one of the most poignant lines in the Scriptures: "But we had hoped"—*sperabamus*, a word of disillusionment and despair. Recall Jim Whitehead's suggestion that in these days a central challenge of leadership is to help people grieve over the loss of familiar assumptions, ways of being together, and traditional patterns of authority.[12] We are not simply grieving a lost past, however; we also are grieving a future which we had once dreamt about, for even that future is not what it used to be! We know much of the past is not worth grieving, but our dreams are another matter.

The vocation crisis, interpreted thus, invites disciples at the crossroads to compassion: to appreciate the sufferings of these colleagues in ministry, to be sensitive to their pain, their confusion, their lack of direction. It invites us to try to love rather than to corner; to invite to the journey without brow-beating; to recognize and accept the limits and the weakness of others as well as of ourselves. We don't step over these folks or walk around them, we bring them with us on the journey or there is no budging at the crossroads.

2) Another concern which confronts us at the crossroads is that which is euphemistically labeled the women's issue: feminism. I believe that all of us, or nearly all of us, are convinced intellectually that the issue of women's equality is a serious justice question.

It is hard to believe that the first Women's Ordination Conference was held in Detroit only fifteen years ago, because it seems that issues of women's roles in Church and society have been around for much longer. Why, I ask myself, does it seem that we have made little headway? I refuse to believe that eliminating sexist language is any longer enough. I contend that just as we have to say: "Vocation crisis, for whom?" we need to ask regarding feminism, "What are we afraid of?"

That very interesting question prompts yet another question: who is "we"? It may be easy enough for us to say that "we" is Rome, or the bishops, or all men, or unregenerate women . . . and in passing the buck we can blame others for resistance and the slowness of change. I have a suspicion, however, about feminism. It is that all of us, even the most ardent feminists, have some fears. And until we voice our fears aloud there will be no progress in confronting this issue at the crossroads.

What are we afraid of? I cannot tell you what you are afraid of. I can tell you what some of my fears are:

I am afraid of the very word *feminism* because it is such an umbrella word and a catch-all for an enormous agenda, some of which I cannot subscribe to. All of us stand at some place on the continuum between Mary Daly and Phyllis Schlafly, but we keep our cards very close to our chests.

As a student of worship, the more I study the more I recognize the role that sexism and patriarchy played in shaping the tradition and I recognize how women's insight and experience were systematically censored out of the community's prayer. But as a liturgist I am afraid of undermining the community's traditional patterns of worship or attempting to recover women's experience because of the fiercely conservative nature of worship itself and because of the mistakes which will inevitably be made in welcoming and incorporating women's memory when we make our anamnesis.

I have come to recognize that much of our language is no longer adequate to name my experience of God, yet I am afraid to lose the God of my childhood, the God who has served me well. I know that the way I name God makes me take or avoid responsibility for creation and human life, makes me child or adult, makes me whole and human or inferior in the pecking order, makes me wonder if I will ever image God or tells me that I am called to that task right now, today.

As a professional woman in the Church I have been the object of overt and covert sexism, of being marginalized and made to feel not part of the club. Yet I am afraid that if I make waves I will become more marginalized and lose the regard of my colleagues and the perquisites and privileges of membership. For membership in the club, as American Express reminds us, has its privileges.

I am also a professional educator, a good teacher trying, in the face of success, to adapt new feminist methods of pedagogy, yet I wonder and I fear that I may lose my touch as a teacher in making this transition.

I am afraid for the Church of the future as some of my closest associates and friends decide that they cannot remain within the community. I am afraid that the Church will not respond quickly enough, that it will become more and more irrelevant in people's lives. I wonder sometimes what keeps me loyal, and I wonder whether my very loyalty is not part of the problem.

The name of my fears is "legion." What are you afraid of? Why can't we talk about these issues, and by talking disarm our fears and give one another the hope we need for a new vision of Church at the crossroads? We will construct a new future, we will transform our fears into hopes by seeing through the present to hints of God's glorious future—but we will do it together or not at all.

3) What are our choices as we stand at this threshold? Last October, Nathan Mitchell concluded an *Assembly* editorial on "Ministries Today: Service or Status?" with these words: "In a church that has long overvalued the 'status' of the ordained, there are welcome signs that the call to discipleship, the giftedness of *all* the baptized, is a more important issue than who gets to sit in the big

chair at Mass."[13] I heartily concur with this sentiment, as I add my own concern that there may even be a new race to the big chair in so-called "priestless" celebrations.

The leader of prayer is always and only Jesus Christ, our high priest, who stands before the throne of grace interceding on our behalf. That is the essential consideration we must bring to a discussion of presidency. But more is at stake in the new debate about "priestless" or, more aptly, "Eucharistless" celebrations, as we await the publication of the document *Order for Sunday Celebrations in the Absence of a Priest.*

While the regular celebration of liturgy may leave little time for stepping back, nevertheless we stand at a critical juncture in this journey we make as a pilgrim Church. It is a time for reflection and discernment.

The implementation of this document touches upon a number of important issues: the sacramentality of the Church; the appropriate ordering of the assembly; the regular celebration of the paschal mystery; the unity of time, event, and community (the tradition of Sunday); the potential for confusion (folks who prefer "Sister's Mass" because it is shorter or better prepared); the possibility of even more alienation for priests who will be turned into visitors—even strangers—in the assemblies they are asked only occasionally to lead; the potential for the Eucharist to become once more an object rather than an action which we do together; the postponement of the underlying issues of gift and grace for leadership in the assembly.[14]

We must consider the long-term ramifications of each and every expedient short-term solution. At this juncture, and in light of the weighty questions posed by so-called "priestless Sundays," non-reception of the *Order of Sunday Celebrations in the Absence of a Priest* seems to be the only thoughtful option for disciples at the crossroads. Rather than celebrating Word and Communion services, perhaps we may choose to gather for Morning Praise or for a Service of the Word. Fasting from Eucharist will allow us time for the necessary discernment which these questions deserve. Fasting from Eucharist may also serve as a catalyst to address the deeper issues named above.

For those who find themselves on thin ice, there is always the possibility of retreating to the safety of the shore where the ice is thicker. Retreat is a choice. So is disillusionment, defeatism, or paralysis. None of these choices, however, is life-giving, nor is cynicism or anger with the Church.

One may choose to grieve, to grieve the past which is no more as well as the future which we once imagined and upon which we built our hopes. Grieving will make room in our hearts for new hopes and new dreams.

One may choose to embrace and use power and authority appropriately (perhaps in an understated way, if this is what our times demand) for the sake of healing and building up the Church in faith and love. I have, in this paper, implicitly suggested three virtues which might characterize leadership, moral authority, and integrative power at the crossroads: compassion rather than anger, hope rather than fear, and discernment rather than expediency.

One may, finally, choose to *live* the paschal mystery. Liturgical ministers talk about it a lot and celebrate it continuously. Now, at the crossroads, we may choose again and with one another to live in the shadow of the cross of Christ, and from there to announce the reign of God: that the sick are cured, the dead raised, the leprous healed, the demons expelled; we know it to be true for they are us, disciples of the Risen One, ready to give what we have so freely received.

In conclusion, I offer a blessing for disciples at the crossroads:

May God sparkle in all of us
    as sunlight upon water,
May we radiate for each other
    compassion and hope,
May our work be fruitful,
    our joys profound,
    our pain redemptive,
May our discipleship be rooted
    in the very life of God.
May we be for each other,
    for family, for friends,
    for those in need,
    for those especially
        whose faith has come to staleness
        and whose hope has died
    —a burgeoning ALLELUIA
    —light and peace and simplicity

Disciples at the Crossroads: Where Do We Go Now?

—full gratitude, full openness.
May we take nothing less for granted
than the life we seek
to build up in common.
May we suffer the pain of a
fully generous love.
May we remain steadfast
in the shadow of the cross,
And rise to meet the passion
of this world
Relying always
on the untiring good Spirit of our God.[15]
Amen.

NOTES

1. Michael Buckley, "'Because Beset with Weakness . . . ,'" *To Be A Priest: Perspectives on Vocation and Ordination,* eds. Robert Terwilliger and Urban T. Holmes (New York: The Seabury Press, 1975) 125–32.
2. John Shea, "The Prayer of the Holy Sacrifice of the Mass," in *The Hour of the Unexpected* (Niles, Ill.: Argus Communications, 1977) 76–77.
3. Hebrews 2:18; 4:15; 5:2.
4. Buckley, "Beset with Weakness."
5. See Sandra Schneiders, "The American Culture—Helps and Hindrances Regarding Collaboration," in *Newsletter of the National Organization for Continuing Education of Roman Catholic Clergy* 12 (1984) 25–39.
6. Rita Maginn, "Lay Ministry in Transition," *R.S.C.J.: A Journal of Reflection* 10 (1989) 142.
7. *Called and Gifted: The American Catholic Laity.* Reflections of the American Bishops commemorating the fifteenth anniversary of the issuance of the "Decree on the Apostolate of the Laity" of Vatican II, November 13, 1980, 30.
8. Maginn, "Lay Ministry."
9. See Lawrence Cada et al., "The Life Cycle of a Religious Community: A Sociological Model," in *Shaping the Coming Age of Religious Life* (New York: The Seabury Press, 1979) 51–76.
10. See Richard McBrien, "The Church at the Crossroads," elsewhere in this volume.
11. See Eleanor Bernstein, "Introduction," elsewhere in this volume.
12. See James Whitehead, "Worlds of Scarcity: Promise of Abundance" elsewhere in this volume.

Kathleen Hughes, R.S.C.J.

13. Nathan Mitchell, "Ministries Today: Service or Status?" *Assembly* 16 (1989) 457.

14. See John Baldovin, "Liturgical Presidency: The Sacramental Question," elsewhere in this volume, for a development of the theological foundation of these concrete concerns.

15. Sharon Karam, "Blessing," *R.S.C.J.: A Journal of reflection* 8 (1987) 60 (adapted).